"I want to recommend Kim Ketola's book Crad
directly with the pro-life movement over the last few years, I have seen the
incredible need for a book such as the one you hold in your hands. Through
powerful, real stories, many of them from her own life, Kim graciously
communicates the love and hope Jesus brings to hearts wounded by abortion.
May God continue to bless and lead your ministry, Kim!"

—**Rebecca St. James**, singer, author, actress

"The estimated one in every five Christian women who have experienced
abortion will experience the love of the Lord through this beautiful, insightfully
written book. Kim relates stories of those with broken hearts who encountered
Jesus, and she bravely shares her own experience of repentance and meeting
his comfort and healing after abortion to deliver a personal, intimate, and
hope-filled read and resource."

—**Peggy Hartshorn, PhD**, president of Heartbeat International

"A compelling, powerful, honest account of accepting forgiveness and
experiencing the miraculous, healing power of God. Kim uses clever, modern-
day retellings of biblical encounters with Jesus that clearly illustrate his love
and compassion, and she gives true-life testimonials that provide a deeper
understanding of grief and its consequences. Biblical reflection and useful
action steps help readers better understand God's love and true healing. A
powerful reminder that God wants to redeem pain in our lives and use it for
his glory."

—**Dr. Wess Stafford**, president and CEO of Compassion International,
and author of *Too Small to Ignore* and *Just a Minute*

"With candid honesty, Kim Ketola helps readers heal from the suffering after
abortion. Prayers and practical steps at the end of every chapter provide
guidance in transforming hurt into hope. And thoughtful reflections and
biblical insight help readers find Christ's restoration the minute they open their
hearts and give him permission to forgive and heal."

—**Theresa Burke, PhD**, author of *Forbidden Grief*, and
founder of Rachel's Vineyard Ministries

"Kim Ketola's discerning creativity translates biblical stories into practical help
for those struggling after abortion. Sharing her personal walk from shame to
new life, she writes from the heart and offers hope, forgiveness, and help for
strengthening faith in this awesome book!"

—**Georgette Forney**, cofounder of the Silent No More Awareness Campaign

"*Cradle My Heart* is like the steady hand of an empathetic physician doing heart surgery with truth and love. You bring the grief. Let God supply the grace."

—**Rev. John Ensor**, author of *Answering the Call: Saving Innocent Lives One Woman at a Time* and executive director of global initiatives for Heartbeat International

"The emotional aftermath of abortion is rarely talked about with such honesty and compassion. As Kim courageously shares her pain and path to healing, you will be encouraged, filled with hope, and reminded that nothing separates you from the love of God."

—**Linda Mintle (PhD, LCSW, LMFT)**, speaker, professor, and best-selling author of *Letting Go of Worry*

"With keen insight and courageous authenticity, Kim Ketola reflects on her haunting experience with abortion as a springboard to encourage others to process their similar experiences. Through dawning observations—as insightful as they are brief—Ketola puts words to the unspeakable and gives expression to the inexpressible. She encourages readers toward brutal honesty and liberating grace—or perhaps it is brutal grace and liberating honesty—to create chapters that insist upon scriptural reflection and prayerful response. No reader is too wounded or wretched or worldly or wise to gain something from this book. For no reader lives in a place untouchable by an encounter with the Lord of life."

—**Douglas S. Huffman, PhD**, Professor and Associate Dean of Biblical & Theological Studies, Talbot School of Theology

"As a Christian psychotherapist who works with abortion-related trauma, I highly recommend this compassionate work that differentiates the need for spiritual from emotional healing, and moves the reader in a personal way from a place of shame to grace like no other book out there on this topic."

—**Gregory Hasek, MA/MFT, LPC**, executive director of Misty Mountain Family Counseling Center; adjunct professor at George Fox University

"A powerful mix of Scripture, personal testimony, illustration, and practical action steps for each chapter. These insights show the power and love of Jesus to restore and give future hope. If I were still preaching, I'd order a case of these books and leave them in a semi-private place where women could unobtrusively pick up a copy—and I recommend my pastor friends do just that."

—**Don Miles, EdD, MDiv**, mental health professional, pastor, and board member of Living Free Ministries

"*Cradle My Heart* shows Kim's insight and heart of compassion through a beautiful parallel of biblical truth and practical application which will both comfort and encourage. Even after abortion, God's grace increases all the more."

—**Jimmy Ray Lee, DMin**, President of Living Free

"Two perspectives make this book meaningful: Kim's empathetic personal journey to healing, and Jesus Christ's grace and truth. Kim makes his encounters with the infirm and helpless both personal and relevant, sure to make a difference in many lives."

—**Rev. James Lamb**, national executive director of Lutherans for Life

"I've known many tragic stories after abortion from the anonymous, who came to me in confession or for counseling, and some who attempted, or even tragically completed, suicides. Kim's book will open the hearts of the children of God who need to know that our Lord loves all and forgives all who ask."

—**Rev. Robert McKewin**, retired

"Well researched and scripturally rooted, *Cradle My Heart* is an excellent resource for any post-abortion ministry. Women who carry the cross of abortion will find a compelling and convincing read because Kim has been where her readers are. Her meditations remind us that Christ's mercy is greater than our weakness, and so we find the courage to be at peace with ourselves and to help others on this painful journey."

—**Father Frank Pavone**, Priests for Life

cradle my heart

Finding God's
LOVE
After Abortion

Kim Ketola

Foreword by Ruth Graham,
President of Ruth Graham and Friends

Kregel
Publications

Cradle My Heart: Finding God's Love After Abortion
© 2012 Kim Ketola

Published by Kregel Publications, a division of Kregel, Inc., P.O. Box 2607, Grand Rapids, MI 49501.

The author and publisher are not engaged in rendering medical or psychological services, and this book is not intended as a guide to diagnose or treat medical or psychological problems. If medical, psychological, or other expert assistance is required by the reader, please seek the services of your own physician or certified counselor.

Details in some anecdotes and stories have been changed, and in some cases are composites of real individuals whose true stories are representative of actual events, in order to protect the identities of the persons involved.

Library of Congress Cataloging-in-Publication Data
Ketola, Kim, 1954-
  Cradle my heart: finding God's love after abortion / Kim Ketola.
    p. cm.
Includes bibliographical references.
1. Abortion—Religious aspects—Christianity. I. Title.
HQ767.25.K48   2012   363.4'6—dc23   2012019247

ISBN 978-0-8254-3928-5

Printed in the United States of America

13 14 15 16 17 / 6 5 4 3 2

To my family,
On earth as it is in heaven

In all their distress he too was distressed,
  and the angel of his presence saved them.
In his love and mercy he redeemed them;
  he lifted them up and carried them
  all the days of old.

Isaiah 63:9

Contents

Opening Eyes and Hearts

When our Ruth Graham and Friends Conferences needed someone to address the abortion issue with sensitivity and grace married to biblical truth—someone not afraid to speak the truth or confront the hard questions, someone who knows firsthand the loving touch of God's healing and restoration for her own life—Kim Ketola became that someone.

She has touched many lives at our events as she presents God's truth with relevance regarding abortion. She is sensitive and loving, but doesn't back down from the truth, even when it is painful. With gentle, loving discussion she addresses an issue carried far too long in shame and denial.

In *Cradle My Heart*, you will see this same spirit. You will experience release, and encounter wholeness that only comes from God's forgiving touch. Too many people in our culture treat abortion as a political, medical choice. It is far more. Kim Ketola takes this issue away from politicians and doctors and elevates it tenderly to a spiritual level to open eyes and hearts to the amazing grace and redemption of a loving heavenly Father.

—Ruth Graham, author of *In Every Pew Sits a Broken Heart*,
daughter of Billy Graham, and president
of Ruth Graham and Friends

At the Heart of Things

Abortion is such a hot-button issue. Politics, women's rights, privacy, and medical practice all come into play. But after you experience it, the questions become much more personal, much more pressing.

For me, abortion became a spiritual issue, a matter of the heart.

If you're reading this book after an abortion in your past, you may feel apprehensive: *Will I be judged? Will this really help me heal or make me hurt worse?* You don't want others to know. You may sense that Christians opposed to abortion would reject you for having had one (or perhaps more than one). Even if it's now years later, in your heart, you're still unsettled because of questions too difficult to face.

My most troubling question became this: *Where did my faith go?*

As a little girl and then as a young woman, I always believed in God, though I never fully understood all the teachings of the church. My young mind just didn't get it. I knew God required reverence in church. I learned to confess my wrongs. I prayed some, especially in times of trouble. But abortion brought the worst trouble into my life I had ever known, and I couldn't see how to set things right with God. My faith was so frail and fragile that, even though somewhere in my heart I always knew it was true, I just couldn't believe God loved me no matter what. Instead, I wrestled endlessly with my questions and my doubts:

How can I face myself knowing what I went along with or willingly chose?

Does God hate me?

Was it a baby? When does life begin?

How do I manage these painful feelings of shame and worthlessness?

Can I be forgiven—and must I forgive?

What about the baby in eternity? What about my eternal destiny? What about heaven and hell?

If I share the truth with others—won't they reject me because of what I've done?

Will this sorrow ever end?

Is it really possible to just start over with God?

You may have other questions or strong emotions right now, such deeply private feelings that even picking up this book was a difficult thing to do, especially if you feel you were coerced or forced to abort.

I can't know your situation. I do know from talking with hundreds of others who have experienced abortion too, that while there are no two stories alike, there are common feelings and shared sufferings. You'll find some facet of your story here. We find ourselves in each other's stories somewhere. Every story has helped me see the possibility of a glorious spiritual renewal in Jesus Christ. He brings the promise of hope. He gives new life. Our loving God has placed everything in Jesus' hands (John 3:35). This means he will even join you in your sorrow. He will cradle your heart in his love.

I found this to be true. Where once there was a spirit of despair, now there is a quiet faith. Where there was mourning, now there is praising for God's mercy. Guilt has given way to grace, and shame has melted into freedom to sing and shine and enjoy life to the full.

This freedom I've found can be yours too. I hope to help you grasp God's promise of this. I want you to start now by imagining a place of peace with him after abortion . . .

Can you see it? Every troubling question is answered and every longing for freedom from grief and guilt is satisfied. Here, you find forgiveness, family restoration, hope, and joy. Even after abortion, God gives new life.

It's so important to learn that you are not alone. You are not the only one.

In fact, one-third of women in their mid-forties have had abortions.[1]

Every year, more than 1.3 million women experience elective abortions. And nearly two-thirds of these women have some Christian religious affiliation.[2] Based on these statistics, I believe there are 8 to 10 million Christian women who, like me, never held the baby they thought they did not want, but now wish they could have known and loved.

The numbers are huge, but there is no comfort in knowing so many suffer, only in how many can be freed from abortion's scars as one-by-one we each find the comfort of knowing Jesus Christ. He is our champion, the captain of salvation (Heb. 2:10 NKJV). He comes in friendship, lending his power for living, offering his help in laying down our sorrow and struggles and pain, and extending his welcome into the full benefits of being in God's family.

I know it can be hard to find Jesus after abortion. But in every chapter of this book you will meet him at work helping people with struggles like yours: a man whose crippled faith lay dormant for decades, a woman thirsty for something or someone worthy of her worship, another woman whose sinful lifestyle led her horribly astray, a money-centered man who later gave it all away, a pair of loving sisters grieving a beloved brother, a disgraced leader whose honor was restored. These encounters and others show real people who met Jesus and walked away forever changed. He healed them all, and he heals us still.

For help in healing, you'll find three practical tools at the end of each chapter:

- REFLECT. Reading God's promises in the Bible will remind you of his love and providence, and the selections listed here will help you strengthen your faith and find confidence in reading his Word for yourself.
- REQUEST. A prayer helps you begin your own loving conversations with Jesus.
- RESPOND. Nurturing exercises and steps guide you to live in a healthy relationship with God every day—the very essence of all spiritual growth. There are even some suggested songs for you to sing as you start a whole new sound track of your new life.

So, are you ready to entrust Jesus with your heart?

The truth is Jesus already knows your every thought and everything about your past. He has heard your every secret and is intimately familiar with even your hidden faults—and he loves you. He loves you in spite of what you've done and because of who you are. He promises: "Never will I leave you; never will I forsake you" (Heb. 13:5), and "whoever comes to me I will never drive away" (John 6:37). And he asks simply this: *Are you willing to begin a new life now?*

Part One

Your Heart

An Examination

Do you want to get well?

When an abortion in your past has stopped you from living in peace and wholeness, and crippled your sense of spiritual freedom, Jesus reaches out with God's love to stir us and move us forward. He helps us to pick up right where we are and begin again in life.

I learned this, but only after many years of feeling spiritually crippled. After an abortion, I sensed I'd lost something valuable and precious, but I couldn't discuss the loss with anyone. Who could possibly understand? How could anyone know the depth of responsibility I felt (or how deeply I blamed others) for making a mess of my life?

I found it difficult to reach out to God. Maybe you too believed God didn't want to help you out. You may wonder how God could have let this happen to you. How can you possibly move on and overcome the past?

Jesus doesn't provide an answer outright; instead he asks a question that speaks directly to our hearts.

The Last Thing on My Mind

When I chose abortion, I didn't first ask myself about whether it was morally right or wrong. That was literally the last thing on my mind. I wasn't thinking about all the moral considerations as much as how being pregnant and having a baby would change my life. I weighed the scant conversations while planning the procedure:

> *"No, it's not a baby. It's just tissue."*
> *"Yes, it's very safe and confidential. No one needs to know."*
> *"You can go through this, and it will be as if you were never pregnant."*

These whispered deceptions cloaked my decision as what people call "reproductive choice." No one would need to know I was sexually active. No one would need to know my shame and rejection over my fiancé's refusal to proceed with our plans to marry. No one would need to know I was building my career and my future on a hidden lie.

The conversations on the day of my abortion were even shorter.

> *"No, I don't have any questions."*
> *"Yes, we will pay cash."*

Resignation and detachment covered a sadness I didn't reveal, even to myself. *We'll never get married now. My life is up to me.*

I just wanted to get there, get through it, and get out. I made no eye contact and kept my head down. I managed to stay emotionally detached until immediately before the procedure. Then, in a terrible moment, I knew without a doubt that what I was about to do was wrong.

The attendant had grasped my hand and asked, "Are you all right?"

The physical contact and a kind tone in her voice woke me to the reality of what I was about to do. I knew in my heart it was wrong. I knew I should just say, "Stop!"

Instead, I lay silent, witnessing my own failure and fear. After a while, I nodded for her to continue.

She then called my attention to a jar affixed to a tube and equipment off to the side. She said this jar would signal the doctor, who remained out of view, that the procedure was complete.

There was noise. There was pressure. I watched the bright red jar. And thus ended the life of my little one.

Paralyzed by the Past

After abortion, you may know in your heart that you have done something terribly wrong or suffered a terrible wrong. But the past is past. You probably think, *What can I do about it? No one can help me now.*

Those kinds of thoughts can be paralyzing. That's not some fatal flaw in you. It's natural, normal. The law of inertia says an object in a state of motion (or rest) tends to remain in that state until an external force is applied. Gravity forces an object to fall and momentum makes it move. Abortion can put you in a spiritual inertia—feeling stuck, depressed, numb, unable to befriend or love with any intimacy. You feel so far from God that your lame spirit renders you helpless and immobilized, as happened to one man for thirty-eight years.

This man lived in a big city, alive with activity, as always happens before a big holiday. People were wrapping up business, finalizing preparations, making their way to church—and most of them were going out of their way to avoid contact with the man on the street corner in a broken wheelchair. He had become a fixture there, just across the street from this prospering big-city church. People even referred to him as Wheelchair Man—a daily presence in the park, near a pond where the crippled, afflicted, and down-and-outers sought the only refuge the city had to offer.

A well-dressed mother pulled her daughter close as they approached. Wheelchair Man smiled at the child. But when she returned the silent greeting, he overheard the little girl's mother hiss, "Don't talk to the homeless guy."

He wasn't homeless, but he was getting used to people making that mistake. He actually came from a good home. Of course that was long ago, so long past that he was beginning to forget what that meant. He was becoming accustomed to people treating him like trash strewn along the road. But the holidays reminded him in glimmers of the good life he'd thrown away by his own poor choices. *It's just as well that decent people avoid me,* he thought. *I can't stand to look them in the eye anyway.* He was tired of seeing the disdain and sometimes fear. So, instead, he stared at the pond. Local legend said those waters held healing. He

wanted to believe that, needed to believe it. He seldom glanced at the
church anymore either. Somewhere in his heart, he believed in God,
but the shadow of that building seemed to chill him even more than
the icy people passing by. Was God really that close, and really that far
away?

Today was like all the other holidays past, so he focused on the waters. Intent on waiting for them to stir—as legend said they would when
a healing was about to happen—he missed a group of men getting all
too close. Now they were near and that meant trouble. Guys like this
usually decided he must be loitering and made him bear the brunt of
their scorn.

Are they talking about me? he wondered.

A fragment of their conversation hung in the air: "Thirty-eight
years . . ."

He sighed. They were definitely discussing his case. He'd been here
thirty-eight years. Everyone knew it. *Well, let them talk,* he decided. *It's
not like I can escape with a broken wheelchair. I would have thought people
would be tired of talking about me by now. I never admitted to anything, but I
guess my life here in the land of the lame tells the tale.*

One of the men stepped forward, walking straight toward him.

He must be their leader.

But something was different about this fellow. He didn't turn away.
He bent down and peered straight into the lame man's eyes. "Do you
want to get well?" he asked.

If there wasn't such gentleness in this man's eyes, in his voice,
Wheelchair Man would have thought this was some kind of a sick joke.
*Of course I want to get well! Why else would I subject myself to public ridicule
by living at the edge of this pond with my disability on full display for almost
forty years?* Yet something kept him from answering—screaming, "Yes!"
Was it pride? Was it shame? He was confused. *Maybe this stranger doesn't
know these waters have healed many people. Maybe he doesn't know I'm here
out of desperation.*

"The waters," he struggled to explain, "the waters can heal, you
know. But my wheelchair is broken. I have no one to help." Even as he
said this, Wheelchair Man no longer believed he was helpless. He felt a

powerful surge of love directed his way, which suddenly made the pond and his problems seem to fade.

"Get up!" the leader told him. "Pick up your things and walk."

Wheelchair Man felt compelled to stand. He took one step. And then another! He was walking!

But he was walking right into the path of another group, the people who were at the church every single day. He knew they knew him (talk about being a regular!). He knew they had seen his face grow older as they stepped over him year after year on their way to worship. Yet now they acted like it was nothing at all to see him walk. Now, instead of being glad for him, they stopped him and called him out for vagrancy.

Didn't they want to know more about his healing? he wondered. Didn't they see how remarkable this was: thirty-eight years of misery, over in an instant!

No. These people seemed to care only about the law, about catching someone who had challenged their authority in order to keep the corner clean.

To think, I've lived in fear of those guys for thirty-eight years, Wheelchair Man thought. *I've feared them too long.* He glanced back at the leader who had told him to get up, the one who had stopped and looked him in the eye. The leader nodded toward the church. Wheelchair Man smiled. He knew where the real power came from this day. And then he crossed the street and walked inside to give God praise.

Steadied to Walk Toward Wholeness

The leader in that story is Jesus, and until he was able to apply the external force of truth, the man in the wheelchair could never walk in healing grace. No one could help him from that pool of self-pity, that ocean of grief and misplaced faith, but Jesus. There is no hope of being freed from crippling shame, guilt, self-loathing, and condemnation, until Jesus.

Like the paralyzed man, you may have all but lost your faith. You may be going to church or avoiding it, in a private quest for peace and wholeness, for grace. Only Jesus can help you find spiritual well-being by facing an unholy state head-on as his light dawns in our lives (Matt. 4:16).

Look more closely at the story in John 5:1–15. Picture the setting in the holy city of ancient Jerusalem.

Jesus had traveled to Jerusalem for pious observance of a Jewish feast day. Such religious obligations had requirements; a detour to visit the crippled and infirm would render even a priest unholy, ceremonially unclean, and thus unable to enter the temple himself (Lev. 21:17–23). Disabled people were shunned and excluded from community activity, according to *The Jewish Encyclopedia*:

> The blind, together with cripples and lepers, were outcasts of society and kept quarantined outside the town limits; they became paupers and a menace to passers-by. When David besieged the Jebusites at Jerusalem, the blind and crippled mendicants [beggars] were so numerous that he was compelled to take stringent measures against them (2 Samuel 5:6–7). In the eyes of the ancient Hebrews the maimed, and especially the blind, were thought to possess a debased character.[1]

Jesus goes out of his way to love the people others reject as too far gone for God. It was a radical departure for a godly, holy man to visit this pool, yet here Jesus is; here Jesus looks the lame man in the eye and asks him to face the state of his heart. Of course, the lame man of John's gospel is not known for any involvement in abortion whatsoever. But Jesus does indicate in John 5:14 that this particular man's physical debilitation was related to personal sin—maybe even blaming others for failing to help him get into the pool for healing. But Wheelchair Man had bigger problems. Those of us who turn from faith instead of toward it when we've experienced a crippling blow in life have bigger problems. Only Jesus helps us face the complacency that holds us back. Only Jesus can restore any of us excluded from the church to full participation by removing whatever stigma of affliction we suffer. Only Jesus can heal.

Why Not Get Well?

After abortion, we are afflicted. We are waiting at a pool of betrayal or self-pity, or beside a sea of self-loathing and regret. We feel dejected and trapped: *I wish I could go back and undo everything, but it's too late for that now.* Jesus asks, "Do you want to get well?" (John 5:6). In other words, *do you want to be free from suffering in your spirit and your soul?* This is no theoretical question. Jesus wants you to mark off the limits of your faith. He's asking, *Do you want a new life now?* He's not asking if you believe in a new life. No, he's asking, *Do you want it?*

That question is stunning. Think about it.

Have you taken on affliction as a way of life?

A young bride had been forced to abort following physical violence by her brutal husband that left her hospitalized for a full week receiving care for bruises and broken ribs. At age seventy-five, the woman still suffers from this primal wound to her spirit, though decades have passed. She's allowed pain and unforgiveness to define and limit her life. She is especially bitter toward a priest who hurt her by giving poor counsel while she was still recovering in the hospital from the physical battering. Ask yourself if you are nurturing your hurt instead of allowing God to heal your heart. Affliction as a way of life says, *I will never forgive, I will never get over this,* or I *will take this to my grave.*

Do you vaguely desire new life, but don't want to change?

Wanting life to be different and wanting to change are not the same thing. Change takes effort and commitment. You know you'll have to work on addressing problems, but you wonder if you're up to the task. You may worry more about what others will think than you do about pursuing peace of mind. You may feel too defeated and debilitated to move. Have you ruled out getting help from a pastor, priest, or spiritual counselor? Affliction says relief is out of the question, no matter how much you may wish you could feel better.

Have addictions or poor coping skills fogged your ability to choose healing?

One woman reflected, "I just decided there was nothing good about me after abortion. So I sank lower and lower in my behavior and in the type of people I hung out with." Addictions, drug use and other risky behaviors, and questionable associations are all red flags that your judgment might be impaired. Would you consider attending a recovery support group or abstaining from substance use or risky relationships in order to get closer to God? Have you already set limits you've failed to keep? Wanting to be well allows us to consider giving up crutches of this kind in order to risk walking on our own again.

Do you prefer to punish yourself as a perverted form of self-love?

Secret anger at our imperfections leaves us mired in depression, incapable of facing failure as a normal part of life. Our hearts sense we cannot remedy our wrongs, and shame is the way we pay the price. We're left helpless with no hope of change. Can you handle criticism? Even from a friend or someone you trust? Before we "die to self," as Jesus puts it, pride won't allow us to accept that everyone's heart reflects good and bad, moral and immoral, loving and selfish traits. If you are a perfectionist, or if the shortcomings of others trouble you deeply, shame may be an affliction you have come to both know and trust.

Do you cherish the pain of the past?

Unacknowledged grief drives an unrecognized reluctance to say goodbye to the abortion experience. Letting go would mean losing something we hold dear. Do your own tears surprise or embarrass you? Do you give yourself permission to experience emotions or are you easily overwhelmed? I'm not suggesting that we should not be deeply sad over the loss of life. But healthy mourning allows us to move beyond anger and despair into a place of quiet peace. Many of us have glimpsed this peace in others, but we are unwilling to risk letting go of our pain because the pain is all we've got.

Are you tired and tempted to give up on getting well?

A continued focus on a failure to do the right thing on the day of the abortion can make you despair of ever getting beyond it. Have you given up on asking God to forgive you because you still don't feel forgiven? It's humiliating to keep confessing only to return to the problem again and again. I've been there, and I know this affliction inside out. I confessed and begged God to forgive me more times than I care to recall. Begging for forgiveness could neither change my desires nor give me a new heart.

So what do you want?

When Jesus asks, "Do you want to get well?" your honest answer reveals your true attitude toward your spiritual affliction. The man at the pool spoke about how he had no one to help him with his condition. Maybe you feel like him. Maybe you aren't yet ready to risk wanting to get well—you feel crippled by isolation, there's no one to help you, and you feel you just can't help yourself.

The lame man had faith, but he couldn't activate it on his own because his focus was way off. Jesus helped him shift focus from things outside his control (other people, his disability) and onto something he could control (his attitude and faith, self-regard, unhealthy dependence on others, and obedience to God's commands). Jesus applied the external force of truth to the physical and spiritual inertia that had weakened the lame man after his sin (John 5:14).

Jesus helps us connect with our deepest desire to be well. This can motivate us to move forward in faith, even after sin has left us weakened and feeling stuck.

TIMELESS TRUTH
Jesus can set faith in motion, even after sin leaves us
weakened and feeling stuck.

The Moment of Truth

I emerged from the recovery room a half hour after the abortion, exhausted physically from the procedure and emotionally by the turmoil of my choice. A new and unfamiliar feeling settled at my core the minute I saw my fiancé in the waiting room. Bitterness. *He pressed me to do this.* Hatred. *This is all his fault.*

When I got home I went straight to bed. I lay there, silent, but unquiet in my heart for the longest time. I felt more alone than at any other time in my life, before or since. I held my own hand in self-pity, trying to recall the only kindness shown to me that day. It didn't help.

In the years that followed, I would return to my moment of truth, that missed opportunity God gave me to stop before following through with that fateful choice. I tried to confront my failure to let the truth influence me. Packed into that pause was the realization that abortion is not simply an idea, a choice, a solution. I was making the conscious decision to end the life of another human being—my own flesh and blood. As much as anything else, I was shocked. In my panic, until I lay there prepped for the procedure, I hadn't even given that life a thought. And worse, my next thought was only of myself.

I had never before experienced such passivity and cowardice. I could only wonder: *Who was I? Why didn't I? How could I?*

I had no good answers. My lack of insight into the workings of my will only added to my silent resolve to bury this secret in the deepest recesses of my heart. My spirit had come to rest in the cold ground of my immoral choice. Instead of protecting and preserving my child, I chose to protect my economic future and preserve my reputation. Only later would I realize that folly: *as if one child could bring about economic ruin, as if destroying a child could lead to peaceful relations with others.* So, though an actual moment of truth had come, my response told me the truth no longer mattered.

This left me feeling worthless and hopeless.

I stayed in that place of despair, stuck in the moral checkmate of being defeated by my own wrong choice.

That's how sin works. You are pulled into a pit of such darkness that you cannot climb out. As both you and your child are counted worthless, you begin to believe that this is true, that you have no inherent worth. If you were like the many millions of women forced to abort by threat of violence or abandonment, the pain of degradation may feel even more acute.

Or, like me, you may have been a young woman with a future to protect, believing you had no choice; this false belief may have also led you to deny what your heart somehow knew was wrong.

Just the Facts

It turns out the details and circumstances of my abortion were what the statisticians would call "just average." The Guttmacher Institute reports that the majority of women who choose abortion are white, unmarried, between the ages of twenty and twenty-four, using birth control, and under sixteen weeks gestation.[2] Like the majority of women who choose abortion, I was single, in my early twenties, and using birth control that failed. My surgical procedure was medically uneventful and I recovered physically.

But what life is "just average"? What is "average" anyway?

My "just average" experience forever changed my life. The relationship that led to my pregnancy and abortion came to an end. The young man who was my fiancé went his way, but through a mutual friend later sought my forgiveness. His life had been changed too. But by this time my heart had grown cold. I would keep going my way as well and follow my plan to support myself and establish a broadcasting career.

It would be years before I would meet another man, settle down, and marry. And it would be God's unmerited favor that we would have two beautiful, healthy children—children who have enlarged my heart and enriched my life beyond measure.

But even the blessing of children did not heal me. More children won't heal you either, whether you were given another chance to give birth after abortion or not. If not, I must say here that I have the deepest, tender feelings for you—our healing is why I am writing this book. As you continue reading, I hope you find full comfort if abortion has led to infertility or other ongoing problems with your health.[3]

I say the blessing of children after abortion is not healing in and of itself because our hearts don't work that way. Other children will bless us and even allow us a healthy outlet for expressing parental love. But that still won't heal the hurt. In my case, having a later planned family and economic stability would suggest abortion had been a good choice. For years, I wondered what was wrong with me that I still needed peace from my past and couldn't accept these results for wholeness. Those who insist that a pregnancy does not define the presence of a baby would deny that what was missing from the picture was my lost child. But my heart knew.

A journal entry from the months following my loss reads, "Coming home to the little ghost . . ."

How could I have known the high spiritual price to pay? I had placed my faith in my relationship, and then in myself, and later in my career. Just like the man in the wheelchair, I was left out on my own. I had no means of moving into God's healing grace.

Every Choice a Separate Need of the Heart

Many of us have become spiritually confused after abortion, thinking we are being punished by God. We are sure that he hates us for what we have done. In our ignorance and fear, we may picture an angry judge, full of punishments that can never be satisfied. But endless condemnation is not part of God's plan for resolving our spiritual crisis. Jesus came to save the world, not condemn and destroy us.

Vicky struggled to believe this. During her abortion, she was told she had twins. "I was shocked to learn there was more than one baby," she says, "but if my boyfriend didn't want one child—" She cannot speak of it more, but to say, "The experience was traumatic and my grief began right away. I chose to ignore the grief in order to survive and continue with my life. I stayed stuck for a very long time."

Vicky needed a double measure of grace. Maybe you experienced abortion more than once and yearn for a double measure of grace too. So many women do. Repeat abortions account for half of all the procedures every year—millions and millions of American women have more than one abortion.[4] They feel, in their own words, they "should have known better" after the first abortion.

No matter what your situation, the healing mercy of Jesus is measureless. The Bible tells us all sin—not just the big ones—separates us from God, and Jesus came to forgive all sin—not just the little ones (Rom. 3:23).

The truth that helped Vicky can help you: "There is now no condemnation for those who are in Christ Jesus" (Rom. 8:1).

There is now no condemnation. What a beautiful promise. That means even if you are grieving more than one child, there is hope ahead. No matter what your situation or issue, there is new life in Christ.

Every choice related to abortion, after all, represents a personal and specific need of the heart. Take, for example, the instance of a very young teenage girl forced by her parents to end a pregnancy even though she may desperately want to give birth. The parents may have offered only two options: abort or leave home. That's not much of a choice for someone so young. Does this girl bear the full accountability for the decision to take a life? Maybe not; though she may be held accountable for behavior that led to the pregnancy—for choosing to have sex. A girl can, and does, feel guilt in failing to protect the child she's lost. Most teens, especially young teens, are unable to influence the decision of whether or not to abort.[5]

What about the mature, married woman, who followed medical advice to be merciful to a child with no predicted quality of life. This mother may deeply mourn the decision. Did she sin? Did her doctors? Only God knows—and only he can heal their hurt.

The same is true for the drug-addicted woman, who overdosed in her eighth month and emerged from anesthesia after an emergency abortion. She wanted this child. Who will relieve her guilt?

Whether or not your abortion was like one of the heartbreaking special cases above, you need only answer one question from Jesus: *Do you want to get well?*

Once you choose wholeness, the love of Christ can put you on the path to freedom. Ask God to help you face your part in the decision to end the life of a child. Yes, others were involved and need to face God too, but for now Jesus calls for you to review your own actions.

Not all mistakes are sinful, and the Bible never forbids us from making mistakes. In fact, it shows us we are human—we will make mistakes. Taking responsibility for your own decisions helps you face the sins embedded in your mistakes, versus becoming embittered over the sins and mistakes of others. You may be bitterly blaming others, even God. When I examined my heart, I realized I had shifted all blame to my fiancé. So when he tried to issue an apology through a mutual friend after we broke up, I threatened to stop speaking with her if she brought up the matter again. Refusing an apology is one sure sign of blame. This spiritual blame game leaves us stuck—just like Wheelchair Man—in pain, but accepting accountability frees us to face our own wrongs in life. As pastor Rick Warren has said, "Blame is spelled b-lame."[6]

The call of Jesus to "get up" is a call to move past the futility of blaming others for the abortion and for being stuck in the past. When I hear him call, I look up to see a loving, smiling Jesus issue his powerful, gentle rebuke, "Do you want to stop blaming others and being weighed down by sin? If so, you are completely free to move on, starting right now."

Jesus won't even allow you to blame yourself. He moves us to a place where we can forsake the past and begin to walk in his grace. And this is what makes it possible to forgive.

A Posture of Prayer

So where was Jesus on that worst of all possible days?

Even though we did not listen, Jesus did not forsake us then any more than now. Moment by moment he has been working to redeem every aspect of that day for our good. The Bible says even when we inflict harm intentionally, God intends it for good (see Gen. 50:20). This glimpse of his character plants a seed of hope that all is not lost and we may yet see some good come from our wrongs or from suffering a wrong.

For some of you, Jesus may have brought a pivotal moment to you as he did to me, when your abortion procedure was put on pause. That brief, action-packed break was God's grace-filled offer to do the right thing. He's always promised to provide us a way out of trouble, especially when trouble tempts us to put faith in ourselves instead of trusting his goodness (1 Cor. 10:13). He comes to correct our hearts when we are about to do what is wrong (Heb. 8:10). Many respond to that grace and decide at the last minute to say no to the abortion.

But even when we don't, his faithfulness remains. The Bible promises, "If we are faithless, he will remain faithful, for he cannot disown himself" (2 Tim. 2:13).

Jesus also came later in the day of my abortion, when I lay there lost and alone in the darkness trying to hold my own hand. He was there, putting me in a posture to pray. He knew that before I could walk into freedom like Wheelchair Man I needed to spend time on my knees. I had so little faith, and it would take many more years before my prayers became real, but Jesus is faithful. In the corner of that procedure room, he looked me in the eye and he made an attempt to give me the gift of greater faith.

Through his faithful love, today I can say, "By the grace of God I am what I am" (1 Cor. 15:10).

This means I'm not who I was.

I'm guessing you're different now too.

But different isn't necessarily whole. Maybe you're feeling stuck in the darkness with an unsettled heart, wringing your hands over your abortion. That is the time to look up. It is a short journey from hand-wringing to hands folded in prayer, from getting on your knees to standing and taking a step. Let the love of Christ help you now find faith to move from one into the other. As you do, remember Wheelchair Man's faith in the healing waters did not cure him, just as faith in religion and attendance at church cannot heal our wounded spirits after abortion. That doesn't mean you should give up on God or stop going to church. It means that you should go, believing in God's power to make you whole. Allow the people of God and those who have your spiritual well-being in mind to become part of God's promise for your healing. Start by showing up to receive God's grace in the company of others who share your faith. Listen to the words of Jesus and follow him in faith.

After he asks, "Do you want to get well?" Jesus says, "Get up! Pick up your mat and walk" (John 5:8). Maybe your abortion anguish has become a comfortable place of refuge in a hostile world of hurt. Jesus says, Let it go. I have a better place for you. I will be your refuge. I will heal your hurts. I will help you walk beyond a pond of wishful thinking onto the solid ground of faith.

—— *Reflect* ————————————————————————

The story of the lame man at the pool of healing is found in John 5:1–15. As you read of their interaction, try to move beyond the stereotyped Jesus and the stereotyped lame man to truly see their faces, their postures, and to picture their hearts.

- "For the LORD is good and his love endures forever; his faithfulness continues through all generations" (Ps. 100:5).
- "'Come now, let us reason together,' says the LORD. 'Though your sins are like scarlet, they shall be white as snow; though they are red as crimson, they shall be like wool'" (Isa. 1:18).
- "Therefore, there is now no condemnation for those who are in Christ Jesus, because through Christ Jesus the law of the Spirit of life set me free from the law of sin and death" (Rom. 8:1–2).

—— *Request* ————————————————————————

Lord Jesus, I want to get well! I want to move from fear and failure into a new life. Help me leave a place of languishing in weak faith. Help me to face myself now after abortion and lay down the pain of the past as I pick up new faith in you. You know the truth. You know each one involved. Help each of us, Lord Jesus. Forgive each one of us as we accept our part, knowing that you can change us beginning right now. Lord, I no longer need to be anchored to sin and wrong choices. Help me to get up and walk away from the past as you fulfill my true desire to be spiritually healthy now. I ask this in Jesus' name. Amen.

—— *Respond* ————————————————————————

- Choose a daily time and place to meet for conversation with Jesus. Kneeling bedside has worked for people through the ages; our place of daily rest becomes a pleasant haven with the one who knows our thoughts even as we sleep. Jesus wants to enter your world, but he will never intrude against your will. Ask the Holy Spirit to come into every aspect of your life.

- Begin listening to God by reading your Bible. If you have trouble comprehending the King James Version, try a new translation. A study Bible like the *Life Application Bible* (NIV) or the *NIV Study Bible* will feature study notes, a word index (concordance), maps, and other helpful features to aid your understanding. Start small by looking up some of the verses mentioned throughout this chapter and read the verse in context. Ask for God to open "the eyes of your heart" (Eph. 1:18–19) to the meaning as you read each passage.

- Singing helps tune you into how much God loves you and what he wants for your life. Start a new playlist or sound track for your life. As you listen to "Untitled Hymn (Come to Jesus)" by Chris Rice, you can sense how Jesus meets each of us at our point of need; "You Alone Can Rescue" by Matt Redman opens with profound questions about our ability to save ourselves or heal our own souls as the song points us to our hope. "On Eagles' Wings" by The Katinas, and "I'm Not Who I Was" by Brandon Heath help me picture the power of Jesus to heal us and restore. If you have a hymnal, take it off the shelf and start reading the lyrics of your old favorites. If you prefer to listen online, you can find inspiring videos of these songs and watch for free on Vimeo, GodTube, or YouTube; or listen with an online music service such as Pandora. Visit a Christian book store or iTunes and listen to samples of other inspiring songs you will want to purchase and keep in a new collection.

- Write about your abortion experience—for your eyes and God's eyes only. Tell the story in light of Jesus' offer to lead you into spiritual health. It may be hard to remember, and you may not yet feel ready to revisit the events. If so, you might list your questions related to God and the abortion experience. Writing is a helpful activity to process difficult events, but if your emotional pain begins to greatly increase or get worse, please do not force yourself to proceed.

- Seek the support of a Bible study group or other Christian friends who can offer you unconditional listening and love. In appendix A you'll find a list of organizations that offer groups for healing after abortion.

An Invitation

What are you thirsting for?

The public abortion debate seems to grow louder year by year, yet after we actually choose it, the silence becomes deafening. We may be free to choose abortion, but discussing that choice often remains taboo. It's so deeply personal. After abortion, we don't want to talk about it—with anyone.

Feeling overwhelmed and angry, I rejected my former fiancé's bid for reconciliation and even warned my friend who suggested I speak with him that she was not to bring the subject up again. She didn't.

But peace isn't merely the absence of conflict. Such anger and hostility take a lot of mental energy to maintain. Soon I turned it all inward. *This is all my fault*, I told myself. *I've made a fatal mistake and what's done is done.* I managed to avoid abortion as a topic on my daily broadcasts even though my job in radio was to be informed and to inform others on news and current events. *Abortion is too controversial*, I reasoned. *The issue is such a downer. It's just a big argument and no one ever wins.* I kept my experience out of the voting booth too, reminding myself, *I'm against it, but I can't tell other people what to do.* If the conversation went to abortion in a group of friends, I excused myself and left, thinking, *I'll lose my friends if they know what I did. I don't want to break down in front of them.*

To choose abortion is to choose silence. We just want to put the whole abortion experience behind us. So we strengthen our resolve to shut down our thoughts and feelings, and opt out of discussions about abortion, even with those who know us best. Choosing silence can also make it difficult, if not impossible, for you to approach God after an abortion, even if you hunger and thirst to be made right with him. Soon the safety of silence becomes a prison for locking away the pain.

Yet you and I are right at the center of what Jesus came to accomplish in spite of what may have occurred in the past, up to and including abortion. Even though a wall of silence shrouds our hearts, leaving us feeling isolated and alone, Jesus comes to us—not to condemn and reject us as we fear (John 3:17), but so he can free us to live another way. He knows our hidden hearts— and that's how he is able to heal us so completely.

Jesus often went out of his way to meet with just one person. In the same way that he helped the lame man find his misplaced faith, Jesus crossed into hostile territory to break through to one bedraggled woman who was all but silenced by the fallout from her misplaced need for love. Jesus broke the rules to help this woman break free from wrong thinking and beliefs, and futile patterns of behavior. He simply entered into her daily life, asked her for a drink, and gave her an invitation she couldn't refuse.

A Thirsty Stranger

A lone man strolled up the hot main street to the only fountain in town. The rising wind blew dirt and debris down the street, and the afternoon sun made this remote, small border town seem even more miserable. He watched as mothers went about their chores, dragging their tired, crying children along. After the busy scene cleared, a lone woman arrived, carrying several empty gallon jugs on straps over both shoulders, in each hand. She glanced his way, then tiredly set down the jugs by the fountain. She needed to fill each one with as much as she could carry.

"Excuse me," the man said. "Could you give me a drink of water?"

The busy housewife stopped still and stared at him. She didn't know this man, and he clearly wasn't from anywhere around here. *Why was he passing through this no-man's-land of a town? And why would he talk to me?* She didn't want to play the race card, but most people of his kind wouldn't give a person like her the time of day. One thing was sure: he seemed exhausted, as if he'd walked a long way.

Her first instinct was to draw back from him and rush home, but there was something about him that caused her to stand still, thinking.

"A person like you wants a person like me to give you a drink?" She asked with obvious disbelief.

"I do, and if you give me a drink of water now, I will give you a stream of life-giving water and you will never be thirsty again."

Her thoughts chased one another: *Living water? What does he mean by that? Is this guy crazy? He must be a little off or something.* Instead of saying what she really thought, she asked, "And just how are you going to give me this water when you don't even have a cup to get some for yourself? To tell you the truth, I wish you could give me an endless stream of water so I wouldn't have to come to town every day to get drinking water. But just how can you make that happen?"

The man looked at her with a surprising tenderness in his eyes.

"Go home and get your husband and bring him to me."

The woman balked. Who was this man? Had he heard all the gossip? "Um . . . I don't have a husband."

"I know you don't," he said gently. "You have had so many relationships."

Now she felt unsettled and defensive. *What did he know of her life anyway?* "Look," she said. "I can see you have some sort of supernatural or spiritual powers to know that about me. But I don't need you to tell me about God. My parents took me to church. My people know about God just like yours."

"I'm glad you brought that up," the man replied, "because all the rules on religion are about to change. What will matter most is what you really believe in your deepest heart of hearts about true love and all your thirsty longing. Even after all the men, all your failed attempts to find love, your life tells me you have never understood what faith in God could mean to you."

Her eyes dropped to the street. She let go of her water jugs. He patted the bench beside him and called her to come and sit down.

"I . . . don't understand how you know me," she whispered. She looked more intently into his eyes. "But I do know God has promised to send a Savior."

"I am the one whose true love you have longed for all of your life," the man said. "I come to satisfy your thirst for someone you can really look up to—someone truly worthy of your trust and adoration. Believe me, I know you. Let's talk."

How Jesus Sees You

He knows you. Christ knows you. It may have seemed impossible to face him, but when you realize he already knows everything about you, like the real housewife of Samaria discovered in John 4:1–42, isn't it easier to just talk?

She opened up about her feelings when she realized Jesus already knew the facts. Can you relate? Maybe you know how she felt when Jesus pulled out of her the whole story of what she had done in the past that had deeply wounded her soul. They didn't discuss abortion—her problem was a weakness for men. Regardless of the issue, Christ's way of reaching out brings me encouragement. The woman of Samaria couldn't face Jesus, so he planted himself right in front of her. He loved her too much to let her stay isolated and silent. So he looked her in the eye and he spoke about the unspeakable.

First he asked her for a drink of water. Doing so was even more re-markable when taken in its historic context. They met at Jacob's well, situated midway between Jerusalem and the Sea of Galilee, a place that had become hostile territory for Jews because Samaritans lived there and commonly practiced intermarriage with idol-worshiping Gentiles.[1] The enmity between the Jews and Samaritans dated back hundreds of years, driven in part by a Samarian who ascended to Israel's throne, wicked King Ahab.

People on both sides of such strife know each other. They know who belongs and who is an outsider. Abortion has created strife which some-times may spill over into the church. Those who are rightly outraged about the loss of life that happens with each abortion may not be sensi-tive to the pain experienced by those who learned the truth too late, or the double pain known to millions of Christian women of having denied what we knew to be true when we chose abortion against our own religious beliefs.[2]

Whether through perceived judgment or my own guilt, abortion made me avoid church. Many women feel like a second-class citizen in church after abortion—caught in the cross fire of abortion politics and personal guilt and shame.

Sychar, where this encounter between Jesus and the woman at the well took place, had become a rundown neighborhood where respectable Jews refused to go. Jesus would have been fully aware that she was no respectable woman. He knows who is living a sinful lifestyle. Some Bible scholars say she lived with a succession of men to whom she was not married, and others say hers was a case of multiple divorces. Either way, people of the time would have expected Jesus, of Jewish heritage, to avoid her or make some reference to her obvious practice of sin.

But his ways are not our ways. Jesus confronts our problems, not our personhood. The story tells us that Jesus arrived in Samaria worn out and thirsty, and so he zeroed in on thirst, first mentioning his and then drawing attention to hers.

When Jesus took on our humanity, he chose to take on the limitations we all face. I used to fear that Jesus hated me for having the needs I couldn't seem to meet in healthy ways, including the need for approval which drove me to try to preserve my reputation when I chose abortion. I don't know if this was a remnant of unmet needs in childhood, but I do know that I was mistaken about how God would judge my heart's cry for belonging and approval from those more powerful than I.

God doesn't hate us for our weakness and our need. He knows that we are frail and in need of his help. Willingly, he set aside his power in order to experience our weakness in his own flesh—so that we could one day see his heavenly glory. Willingly, he approached the woman at the well with her needs in mind.

It was obvious she was drawing enough water for a household, yet Jesus avoided the personal question, "Are you married?" Instead, he offered a subtle, yet powerful invitation to share the truth.

Her honest answer ("I have no husband") gave him the opportunity to provide insight into the root of her problem. Once the unspeakable was spoken, she realized she could talk to him about anything. Then once she started talking to him about anything, there was intimacy with him.

Imagine her initial relief. He knew the truth without her even having to disclose it, and yet he didn't reject her. Instead, he chose to correct her from his love. Jesus talked with her about her thirsty desire for something bigger in life. He looked right past the sin, or rather right into the sin, identifying and answering her deeper need for a relationship with someone to look up to and adore. Perhaps you've heard this brilliant heart-move of his called "Jesus loving the sinner while rejecting the sin." Jesus showed us what that looks like. He initiated a love relationship unlike any this woman had ever known, and his love allowed her to see herself in a whole new light.

In the same way, Jesus is able to help you consider all the circumstances of your abortion and hold you in love as you think it through with him. Even if he didn't love what you did, he never stopped loving you. As you mourned, he mourned too.

A lifeguard doesn't risk his or her own life to plunge into deep waters out of hatred for the one in need of rescue, even if the swimmer foolishly landed in harm's way. Even after abortion, Jesus comes to save us out of love, even when we can't see we are in need.

It is as if Jesus told this woman, "Yes, I am the Savior you've been waiting for." He opened her eyes to the truth about her desires and deepest thirst. He allowed her a completely fresh start as a witness to love instead of as an object of scorn.

It builds our faith to know that Jesus is a true and accurate mirror. Jesus sees us through eyes of love, and helps us to face God in light of all spiritual truth about our own lives and reflect his love to others.

Many in the town believed in Jesus because of her testimony: "He told me everything I ever did."

TIMELESS TRUTH
Jesus sees us through eyes of love, helping us to face God and reflect his love to others.

When Jesus asked a Samaritan housewife into the light of his love, her life was forever changed. Jesus went out of his way and into a questionable neighborhood to speak to a social outcast about her deepest needs for love. He came to her gently, as she was going about her business. His request to join her in her day simply drew her near, just as she was. As he helped her to see herself as he did, somehow everything changed. She gained new respect from others and a position of local leadership. She became a witness to God's love. Her compelling story helped others learn about the hope Jesus brings wherever he goes. Her reputation was completely restored from outcast to outstanding citizen.

Only God could do that. And God longs to do the same for you.

An Offer of New Life

So what if you were at the well that day? What if Jesus met you while you were out running errands in the midst of your chores today? What if he said, *Bring your child and come back*?

Before I knew his love, I would have been flabbergasted that someone so kind was taking an interest in me. But even as I saw there was no judgment, no malice in his eyes, I still might have answered in a way that denied fully disclosing my choice to abort. I probably would have stuck to the facts by saying, "My two kids are in school today."

How honest would you be? What would Jesus say to you next?

In my case, he might say, "Kim, what you have said is true. You have these two children I have given you. But a true and perfect blessing of mine is missing from your life because you chose to deny a child the chance for life when you ended that first pregnancy. Your heart was so far away from me. I tried to reach you that day, but you didn't seem to hear me or know me and so you didn't respond. In desperation, you relied on yourself—you believed you were all alone, and you let that take you to some terrible places you wish you'd never been. Oh, how I wept with you."

I would have admitted then, "He told me everything I ever did."

Your conversation might sound very different. Maybe you were victimized and forced to abort against your will. Maybe you had more than one abortion. Maybe your parents abandoned you as a teenager with an unexpected pregnancy, the deepest trouble you'd ever faced— or you followed the medical advice to abort and have felt sorrow ever since. The pain we face after abortion is not always the result of our own sin. Your trust in God may have been damaged since you were so mistreated and so badly hurt. You may fear God's anger because you understand you were wrong to choose and act the way you did. Maybe you've confessed and confessed with no relief as you have begged to be forgiven.

Keep your heart open to the simplicity of the Samaritan woman's statement even if you don't believe a frank conversation with the Lord can help right now. The weary, thirsty Samaritan woman said, "I have no husband."

Could your acknowledgment of abortion be so simple? Can you now simply say, "I don't have that child"?

Taking this invitation to face abortion as child loss may take all the faith you have. Right now, you can't foresee how anything good is going to come out of this. Your mind may tell you that it's better to leave the past alone in silence because the process seems frightening and you're unsure of the outcome.

Jesus is saying you don't have to see all the way to the bottom of the well to know there is water, living water, there. He asks simply, *Are you thirsty? Will you receive this cup? Will you walk along with me?*

Joni Erickson Tada put it this way, "Faith isn't the ability to believe long and far into the misty future; it's simply taking God at his Word and taking the next step."[3]

The Bondage of Silence

Of course your answer may not seem as easy to voice as Jesus' question. At least it wasn't for Sheila, who kept silent about her abortion for more than half her life.

"I decided to pretend the day of the abortion never happened," she explains. "That way I could fool my mom and myself. I basically turned off all my emotions and acted like that Saturday never happened. I stayed that way for a really long time. I was in high school when I had the abortion and it wasn't until twenty years later that I finally faced it."

But the silence left Sheila feeling dried out, the freedom in life wrung out of her. "You cannot keep the past a secret from yourself," she says.

She was weary from spending adulthood trying to hide the fact that she had been a pregnant sixteen-year-old. She didn't know anyone else who had gotten pregnant so young, even though statistics suggest that yearly almost two hundred thousand abortions (around 20 percent of the total) are performed on girls aged fifteen to nineteen.[4]

When Sheila accepted that Jesus already knew all the details of her abortion, she was able to risk her fear of not being accepted and share the truth with those in her life who needed to know, including certain family members. In the process, she came to see herself anew. She began to thirst more for acceptance from God in living honestly than acceptance from others in covering up her past. She found the courage to have loving conversations with her mother and with her teenage daughter about both the painful experience of abortion in her past and the hope she had now found in God's love.

What worked for Sheila can work for you with time and much prayer, which were what helped Sheila grow in faith. Please don't consider an unsafe risk of disclosing the story of your abortion until you, too, have spent time with God in prayer and established the loving support of at least one other person who fully understands the needs of those who have experienced abortion. As you seek this love and care, you will find there is a nurturing community inviting you to speak the truth that will set your spirit free. (See appendix A for a list of resources including immediate care.)

Facing the truth is never easy—not for the woman at the well in talking about her many husbands, and not for those of us who choose to talk about abortion. It takes the love of Jesus Christ to give us the courage to admit that abortion is the loss of a child. Without the assurance of his love, that is a hard truth to confess. In fact, you may not be able to say this just yet. I couldn't, until I fully and completely trusted Jesus. For more than twenty years, I kept that door of my heart closed. I could not acknowledge the truth and instead continued to believe I had merely, as it's said, "terminated a pregnancy." Such euphemisms and mental tricks also kept me from acknowledging my own pain.

Letting Jesus shine his love into areas of your life now hidden because of abortion marks a subtle but significant shift from self-reliance to dependence on and full trust in God. When we trust and obey Jesus, we gain knowledge of the truth and freedom from the past.

To commit to change does not mean you have to know how to change. The Samaritan woman didn't have to repair her past. Likewise, we just have to stay engaged with Jesus and keep our focus on him. Doing so will banish the deepest darkness the world or we ourselves can create. Corrie ten Boom survived the horror of the Nazi holocaust. The pain of such an assault on body and spirit is simply unimaginable. Yet she came to forgive everyone involved, even the ones who had tortured her sister before her eyes. She said:

> Look around and be distressed.
> Look inside and be depressed.
> Look at Jesus and be at rest.[5]

The world's attitudes toward abortion can leave us greatly distressed; we cannot seek solace from those who endorse and support what we know has broken our families and our hearts. Some in the world may be well-meaning but ill-equipped to help. Trying to work our own way out of the darkness and pain can leave us feeling damaged and depressed; we know we cannot save ourselves from spiritual destruction. All our rationalizations, defenses, and denials only drain us of hope. There is no consolation in *I did the best I could*. All our anguish, angst, and anger only exhaust our meager strength. There is no power to change in silencing your own heart. Only in Jesus Christ can we look at God and find our rest. In him, we also find power to restore hope.

Just as Jesus did with the Samaritan woman, he will do for you. He has already searched out the things that God alone can see: the battle raging in every human heart. Although we may have committed a terrible wrong with abortion, the war within us can come to a peaceful end. Jesus signed the peace treaty with his blood. Isaiah 53:5 says, "He was pierced for our transgressions . . . ; the punishment that brought us peace was upon him." As I said earlier, peace is not merely the absence of conflict. Peace in a time of war always comes at a sacrificial cost. Jesus paid the ultimate price so everyone can have peace with God. As he cradled the heart of the woman at the well, he knew his mission would soon be complete. He knew he would die to save her from all her wrong notions of love and give her the ultimate secure relationship—eternal love with our Father in heaven. Would she believe? Will we?

Keep on looking to our champion who alone can bring true peace. Jesus has paid for that peace. This is the power of his love—peace with God to those who believe. And he always looks at us through his lens of love.

A Polka-Dot Heart

There is a mystery when two hearts touch. A heart-to-heart conversation with a parent, a mentor, or trusted friend can totally redirect our lives. This same phenomenon is at work, amplified and multiplied, when you listen to Jesus with your whole heart. The Samaritan woman listened and left with more than her water jugs filled—her heart was filled with hope again. Sheila faced Christ and poured out her broken heart and Jesus handed it right back to her, whole and mended. She knows that she is forever accepted and loved. I sat with him at the well and understood that my need for recognition has been fully met in Christ. I can speak freely, and I can hear him now. When Jesus speaks from his heart his words are of love with grace and truth. He gives us strength to connect the dots of our present pain with the past.

Each of us has a polka-dot heart. Each of us needs Christ to help us connect the dots. Maybe right now your heart is marred by overwhelming sadness, troubled relationships, and strife. Or perhaps you just feel isolated and numb. One woman poignantly remarked to me that she wondered if her overeating after abortion was an attempt to keep herself looking pregnant. It took me a long time to connect the poor quality of my relationships to my failure to forgive my fiancé and my rejection of the idea of reconciliation. That's not to say forgiving was easy. But with God's help I have forgiven him, and I pray for his peace.

How did I do this? My love for Jesus led me to follow his loving instructions to forgive (Matt. 6:14).

Sheila needed to connect the dots too. Her expectations of the ideal family limited her ability to be close to the family God actually placed her in. As she accepted God's grace toward her less-than-ideal behavior as a teen, she was then able to give grace and ask for it from those she loves.

Begin to read Jesus' words and start the conversation about your life, but don't worry if you don't yet clearly hear his voice. There is no formula for love. You must forge your own relationship with him as you respond to his leading. We can each trust God's promise of a real and vivid relationship to all who truly want it: "I will listen to you. You will seek me and find me when you seek me with all your heart" (Jer. 29:12–13).

We don't need to hide our hearts from Jesus. In truth, somehow we know hiding from him is not even possible. Still, we remain in the shadows after abortion, nurturing our hurt and protecting our secret while inside we are dying of thirst. It is a small step and a giant leap to move from that darkness to admitting your desire to be closer to God. Will you let Jesus lead you there?

He comes to satisfy our thirst for someone we can love with all our heart, soul, mind, and strength. And that's what God wants most from us—that we would find our deepest satisfaction in life in him—that we would offer him wholehearted love (Matt. 22:37).

Wouldn't you truly love for someone to see you exactly for who you are? Wouldn't it change how you get up in the morning and go to sleep at night to know someone knows you so intimately he can tell you everything you ever did and still hold you in love?

Recognizing Your Thirst

Someone does see you for exactly who you are. Someone does know everything you ever did. And he loves you more than you can imagine.

"Who is this?" you may ask, like the woman at the well.

My name is Jesus, he wants you to know.

He sees you not in the bedraggled, dried up, wrung out way you may feel, but as his most cherished creation. He loves you unconditionally, no matter what you've done or what you're in the midst of doing (Rom. 5:8). There is no good thing you can do to make him love you any more, nor any wrong that will cause him to love you any less.

Yet sometimes you cannot even recognize your thirst. You can know your faith is dry. You can be silenced by shame, not daring to enter into the joy of life with God. You just can't bear to face God, knowing how far you've gone by deciding to abort a child. You long to be free, but the memory of the experience remains and grows worse over time, not better.

If you are thirsting after truth, Jesus promises the spiritual help to heal your heart. He even says when we believe in him, streams of living water will flow out to others from us (John 7:38).

But we will have to recognize that this is not self-help.

Many times I prayed God would forgive me even as I withheld the truth from him. I thought I needed to clean up before I could confess. That thought is an idea far outside the free gift Jesus gave when he died as payment for our sin (Eph. 2:8–9). It's like a man who had a natural talent for golf, but his skill was not quite good enough to make par. When a friend suggested the name of a great teacher, the man replied, "I want lessons, but not yet. I want to get better first."

My untrained faith looked a lot like that. My spiritual growth stalled, just like that golfer who never improved his score. Thinking I could clean up my act before going to God kept me stuck in my self-reliant past, believing I had forfeited my right to pray, which is one of the worst lies we tell ourselves after abortion. The truth is, God desires that everyone should pray to him and everyone should belong to him forever (2 Peter 3:9). We simply cannot help ourselves when it comes to sin— and the good news is that we don't have to. That is the meaning of God's grace; it is surprising and unexpected.

It is as baffling as Jesus showing up in Samaria. He should not have been talking with this woman, but he placed himself above these earthly, largely religious concerns for her sake. He invited her to share her life with him. He gave her the treasured gift of God's perspective on her life.

He's offering that to you too. *Are you thirsting for it?* he asks. *Will you drink this cup?*

Each of us who has experienced abortion needs to get free of the past. You may condemn yourself, or fear others will learn your secret. Empty sympathy may have left you feeling worse than before.

Don't despise your thirst. Speak up about it. Ask for water. Go to where you will get it; God knows your weakness. He made you to thirst. He made each of us thirsty. Even when our thirst may seem to get the better of us, Jesus comes to rescue us with life-quenching love.

Begin to think about what it would be like to accept this invitation to have your thirst for justice satisfied, to feel quenched in your longing for your relationships to be open and truly intimate. Jesus went out of his way to meet with just one person—the woman at the well—a real woman with real problems and real needs. Real people experience real change by encountering the love of Jesus Christ.

When Jesus arrives in your life, inviting you to change, you can believe it is "good news!" (Mark 1:15). He comes to lead us into a completely new way of life—a way that is much better, not worse. Do you believe it? What if he sat across from you right now, promising to quench your thirst for something better, for peace? In Jesus Christ, God has revealed his unlimited eternal love—to a Samaritan woman and to every woman silenced by abortion who is willing to answer his invitation to share her thirsty heart.

────── *Reflect* ──────────────────────────────

Jesus' conversation with the Samaritan woman is found in John 4:1–42. As you read, imagine such an encounter with a thirsty Jesus and put yourself in the story as you ponder her responses and their conversation. Now consider the following truths about how well God knows you, sees you, and cares for you; and think about how he may wish for you to respond:

- "The eyes of the Lord are on the righteous and his ears are attentive to their cry" (Ps. 34:15).

- "If anyone is thirsty, let him come to me and drink. Whoever believes in me, as the Scripture has said, streams of living water will flow from within him" (John 7:37–38).
- "Nothing in all creation is hidden from God's sight. Everything is uncovered and laid bare before the eyes of him to whom we must give account. Therefore, since we have a great high priest who has gone through the heavens, Jesus the Son of God, let us hold firmly to the faith we profess. For we do not have a high priest who is unable to sympathize with our weaknesses, but we have one who has been tempted in every way, just as we are—yet was without sin. Let us then approach the throne of grace with confidence, so that we may receive mercy and find grace to help us in our time of need" (Heb. 4:13–16).
- "God is spirit, and his worshipers must worship in spirit and in truth" (John 4:24).
- "This then is how we know that we belong to the truth, and how we set our hearts at rest in his presence whenever our hearts condemn us. For God is greater than our hearts, and he knows everything" (1 John 3:19–20).

—— *Request* ——————————————————————————

Lord, I am thirsty for your love! I desire to love you wholeheartedly. I choose this day to open up my life to you, trusting your love. You know me through and through, and I can really look up to you with all my heart. You know me so well. Please help me bring my life into the light. Jesus, please help me see myself as you do, as I look into the past with you. And Lord, open up your Word to me as I read the Bible. Help me hear your voice as I read and as you teach me to live in a new way. In your name, I ask these things. Amen.

—— *Respond* ——————————————————————————

- Building new relationships takes time. Develop the habit of reading the Bible daily as a rendezvous with your new love, Jesus. Set aside a time and place and put the appointment in your planner as a time for getting to know him and absorbing his teaching. Find the verses listed above and read them in context. Every Bible has a table of contents near the front to help you find the books of the Bible. Try browsing Psalms or Proverbs.

- Listen to an audio Bible during your commute. The *NIV Listener's Bible*, *The Message*, or *The Bible Experience* help bring the Scriptures to life. You can sample many audio Bibles and find free resources for Bible study and enrichment online at www.youversion.com, www.biblegateway.com, or www.studylight.org.

- Spend your movie time with films depicting the life of Jesus such as *The Gospel According to Matthew*, *King of Kings*, *The Greatest Story Ever Told*, *The Messiah*, and *Jesus of Nazareth*.

- Listen to Aaron Neville sing "What a Friend We Have in Jesus" with a soulfully upbeat encouragement to take our troubles to the Lord in prayer. Kathyrn Scott's "Hungry" puts forth the promise that our hunger and thirst for God will be satisfied. Martin Nystrom's "As the Deer" and Kutless's "All Who Are Thirsty" take the words of Scripture from Psalm 42 and Isaiah 55 and turn them into songs of prayer and praise.

- Write a short letter to Jesus to express your response to the statement, "Bring me your child or children and come back." Notice if you experience a new or different level of comfort when thinking about abortion. Take the step now of identifying at least one person you trust who will listen and support you as you continue. If your distress increases, seek help from those who offer confidential and completely private counseling and care (see appendix A for helpful resources).

An Open Conversation

Who are you listening to now?

A s you begin to embrace new life with Christ you may be nagged by questions about the decision to choose abortion. *Was it right? Isn't this just a matter of choice or personal preference? Is abortion a sin?*

At the time, you may not have thought beyond whether the decision was right for you. Everyone close to you, even people of faith, may have reassured you that it was a wise choice, or perhaps it was couched as the lesser of two evils.

Now you wonder. You had doubts then that have never gone away, maybe only grown stronger. The Bible, written centuries ago before women's rights and modern medicine, doesn't even mention the word *abortion* or even its definition, "terminating a pregnancy." How can you know the truth about how God sees it?

I spent years doubting my decision and then doubting God following my abortion. Even as my later marriage began to crumble, I continued both playing God and hiding from God as my heart receded deeper into my hurt.

My internal struggle was part of a much bigger battle—a battle between God himself and our eternal enemy, a battle for our hearts and minds. As a looming divorce added to the weight of guilt for living my life apart from God, I met a friend who helped me understand how God's love resolves all our internal strife over sin. She told me over and over the truth from 1 John 1:8–9—"No one is perfect, Kim. We all sin. Jesus loves you. Once you confess, he is faithful to forgive you and cleanse you from all unrighteousness." Her grasp of God's love broke through and touched my broken heart. At last, more than a decade after my choice for abortion, I found in God's love my heart's true hope.

I want to stand in the place of such a friend in faith for you today. A true and lasting hope is there for you, for all who believe. There was nothing I could do to repair the past. By choosing abortion I had sinned, resulting in terrible, lifelong consequences. But there is hope. Even though I had lost a brutal and costly battle, Jesus has won the war. Jesus died so I would be forgiven of my sins. Jesus loves us just that much.

Maybe you were like me. Maybe you were so far from a life of faith that you didn't stop to ask God about abortion when you made that choice. Maybe you sought counsel from people of faith, and you were led by them to believe abortion was strictly a personal choice. Many Christian women were told by other Christians that abortion is an acceptable choice based on individual circumstances.

In the heat of battle, a time of confusion, when you feel pushed to make a split-second decision that will affect a lifetime, everything depends on who you're listening to.

The Bitter Taste of Doubt

One young bride learned about this early on. She was enjoying a wondrous gift—the perfect home, an idyllic family farm. Her father-in-law had freely given the place to his son—her husband—the deed for the land, and, it seemed, the very sea and sky too! The gift made her feel deeply welcomed and loved in this perfect family circle. She reveled in being a wife. Her husband protected her and daily shared his father's company with her. She had the security of his very clear expectations. He said they could enjoy the ranch house, the livestock, the fields, and streams.

Her only duty was to avoid the tree at the center of the orchard, which the father said provided for their lives. She didn't trouble herself as to how or why. The tree was beautiful, but she had a healthy fear of it. She heeded the warning that death would result from consuming the fruit, though she wasn't exactly sure what death meant, the idea of it in this beautiful place didn't seem so real anyway because everything was so lush and full of life.

Late one afternoon, a slow-moving stranger appeared at the gate. This was her first visitor ever. When he started up a conversation, seeming to know all about her, she assumed the stranger must be a friend. He seemed especially interested in the orchard.

"This is quite a place you have here," he said. "Did the old man really say you two couldn't enjoy all this?"

"Oh no," she corrected him. "This is all ours to enjoy."

The question struck her as odd. This stranger seemed to imply her father was less than generous, when he had given them everything—this beautiful home and creature companions, the plants, and all they could eat. "But he did instruct us not to touch the big tree in the center of the orchard," she added. "The harvest assures our future."

The corners of the stranger's mouth turned up ever so slightly.

Is that a smile? she wondered, then brushed aside how the idea unsettled her.

"The old man's secret is this fruit," he said, nodding to that one big tree at the center. "It is more luscious than anything you've ever tasted. You should try it!"

She looked at the tree. It was beautiful. The fruit gleamed in the sunlight, as if calling to her, as the stranger moved closer to her and whispered, "Come on, look around at this place. You've got it made for life. There's no worry in tasting just one piece of fruit."

As she moved toward the tree, the fruit seemed to grow larger and more succulent. She started to reach out and touch it but remembered the father's instruction. The stranger saw her hesitate.

"It really does look so good," he said, "don't you think?"

She plucked a piece of fruit for herself, thrilled at what was to come. She took a bite and then, turning to her husband, gave it to him to taste as well.

The stranger slipped away and the bride and her husband gulped regret. The fruit wasn't as good as they imagined. In fact, it left them feeling horrible. What had they been thinking? Why had they listened to this stranger instead of the father? The stranger disappeared, but the father who walked with them every day would be back and so disappointed because they took the one thing he asked them not to—and hadn't he already given them everything? Had he ever withheld anything good from them?

Now, as she looks back, the hardships that had come their way since then were too many to count and impossible to bear. Her husband had grown old before her eyes. His labor and exhaustion were now central to their lives. She deeply desired to influence him, but he seemed determined not to listen. The pain of childbearing was only outstripped by the agony of watching one child die at the hand of the other. Much of that was on her shoulders, as she knew only too well.

But all of that was also a lifetime ago now. As she considered the days of their youth, she found she could retrace every misery that had befallen them to the deception and lies of that intriguing enemy who had pretended to be a friend. A bitter taste rose in her throat. How could she have been so foolish to doubt the goodness of their father because that outsider twisted his one simple, clear request?

All the Wrong Voices

It's so easy to take matters into our own hands, just as the young bride took hold of that fruit. From the very beginning, listening to deceiving voices has derailed women's thinking about abortion in particular. Do you recognize yourself in the young bride's story? Do you recognize it is the story of Eve, the very first woman, from Genesis 2–3:16? Do you also notice Eve's adversary, who is also ours? He's there, just out of sight in the shadows.

Unlike the real flesh-and-blood people Jesus encountered to teach and love and heal, Jesus also interacted with a spiritual being, one he called our enemy, the ultimate thief. You may not believe the devil is real, but Jesus certainly did; he knew Satan's intent to steal the soul. Jesus exposed Satan's rivalry with God when he acknowledged God as our Father (Matt. 6:9), and Satan as the father of lies (John 8:44). In essence, Jesus says that Satan's influence as a father in the world is in giving birth to lies. If we accept the lies, we begin to follow Satan instead of listening to and following God.

As the disturbing truth of Satan's presence in the shadow of our abortion comes to light, we begin to see the lies in the deceptive language used for abortion. "Terminating" a pregnancy is not just "removing a blob of tissue" or "triggering a missed period." There was a new human life placed within us. This new human, our growing child, was not just "a part of a woman's body" or "a parasite" to be discarded at will. Calling our child "a fetus" or merely "potential" life could never render our child subhuman, or negate the reality of his or her existence.

Aside from the emotional pain of abortion, Danielle, an African-American woman, feels the added sting of racism. Through tears over the loss of several children to abortion, she reflects, "We were told abortion is a solution to poverty in the African-American community."

A disproportionate number of black women experience abortion, and there is growing evidence that women of color have been targeted by the abortion industry.[1] Danielle saw this firsthand. "Even the black pastors bought into the lie that the abortionist is needed in the 'hood," she says. "Abortion has helped young black men think they're off the hook. My boyfriend said he loved me, but he just stayed back at our place while I was going through one of the worst days of my life."

The Rev. Clenard Childress, author of *No Shepherd's Cry*, affirms what Danielle discerned about black pastors:

> [At least] 1,452 African American children die each day. Yet most African Americans don't know that. They also don't know for every five African American women who get pregnant, three will choose to abort. If you stopped ten African American pastors and asked them that question, I don't think . . . one of them would know.[2]

Childress is now actively helping the black church preach truth and support women in their time of need. (See appendix A for helpful resources.)

It can be devastating to realize we chose to end the life of another human being based on deceptions, half-truths, human wisdom, or even having listened to a leader who counseled from his or her own deception. You know your own story and you may have heard others:

> *"We were an unmarried couple at a Christian college who chose abortion even though we sensed that it was deeply, deeply wrong."*
> *"My parents were so respected at our church that my pastor said I should just quietly abort."*
> *"My denomination says abortion isn't a sin, but I wasn't sure what to think."*

Spiritual confusion and doubt are the weapons our enemy likes best. The devil is not a creative being—God is the Creator of all things. But Satan lives to corrupt the good things God has created. Jesus said Satan was a murderer from the beginning (John 8:44).

Satan's tactics with Eve show us how, from the very beginning, we've been tempted to listen to all the wrong voices about what's good and right for our lives, what choices draw us closer to God or push us farther away. Our enemy is a deceiver who tries to convince us to reject God and stop listening to him. Satan doesn't care about our future or God's truth. His objective is to separate us from God and take us as his captives for eternity. His most effective strategy is to enslave us through his deadly game of doubt. If he can inspire us to question God's care for us, he is willing to twist the truth and sows his seeds of doubt—engaging in character assassination about God's essential good nature and loving heart.

He comes to Eve twisting the truth by misquoting God, "Did God really say, 'You must not eat from any tree of the garden?'"[3] Eve took his bait. She also changed God's words and his instructions. Satan exploited his distorted picture of God by adding to it an outright lie, "You will surely not die!"

In the same way, abortion rhetoric rejects the truth of what God says about the value of every human life with an outright lie, "It's not a life at all!"

But now our hearts know better.

Rev. Childress's initiative to educate pastors demonstrates that women aren't the only ones who are deceived when abortion tempts us to play God. Panic over pregnancy can make women and men, family members and friends, and even spiritual leaders, listen to the lie that abortion will give a woman an easy out from a difficult situation. By endorsing and choosing abortion, we become vulnerable to another of our enemy's trademark enticements:

> *"You will be like God."*

Many voices repeat this temptation:

> *"You must decide for yourself what's right."*
> *"You're the one responsible for making good things happen in your life."*

When I learned of my unplanned pregnancy, I turned to the man who rejected the pregnancy from the onset. My self-image was so low that I didn't fight for deeper conversations or try to get counsel together with him.

My two confidantes were not in a position to give material help and they offered no alternative to abortion. One tried to assuage my guilt by saying, "It's not a baby yet—just tissue." She might as well have said, "You determine when life begins, Kim, not God." Another told me, "It's up to you, Kim. I stand by you either way." She was granting me permission to be like God. So I landed in the hands of those who lied and said there was no child yet at that stage of pregnancy. And I embraced the lies.

Listening to Satan meant Adam and Eve didn't stay true to God, their Father. After they consorted with the father of lies, Adam and Eve hid. God arrived, asking, "Where are you? What have you done?"

I chose abortion without ever listening to the truth I had known all along within my heart. I was already a mother, and I was choosing to do away with an innocent life. I was only able to face having believed this part of the lie many years later, once I knew Jesus never stopped loving me—he just didn't love what I'd done.

Adam blamed Eve, and Eve blamed the stranger. "The serpent deceived me," she said, "and I ate."

Abortion may have deceived an entire generation, but, one-by-one, we swallowed the lie. In the aftermath, we can choose to remain apart from God, hiding and clinging to our naked shame. Or we can choose to listen to Jesus Christ. Listening to Jesus dispels our doubts. In him, God has overcome all deception—not to cast us out but to cradle our hearts in his loving protection and care.

TIMELESS TRUTH
Listening to Jesus dispels our doubts as he cradles
our hearts in his care.

Jesus, Our Example

We never need to be defeated by our sin because the same destroyer who defeated Eve has been defeated for all time. Jesus, our friend and Savior, won the battle.

Matthew 4:1–11 recounts how the Holy Spirit empowered Jesus in the war with Satan, the embodiment of sin and evil. In the Judean wilderness, a dead and lifeless place outside the holy city of Jerusalem, Satan came to Jesus to torment him. Jesus was hungry, exhausted, and utterly alone—just like those of us who found ourselves with an unplanned pregnancy. Satan comes to those hungry for affection, exhausted by worries of how life changes with a pregnancy, at a time when we feel utterly alone, and he whispers lies.

But we are not alone, Jesus shows us.

The encounter between him and Satan is no different than that between Eve and Satan, or a woman contemplating abortion and Satan. In every scenario Satan tells lies as he tries to make one doubt God and to act upon that mistaken belief. When Eve was being deceived, her real needs surfaced. Would God meet her physical hunger, and could her desires be fulfilled in him? And what of her need for autonomy and significance—to be like God? Satan attacked Jesus the same way—physically, mentally, and spiritually. At every onslaught, Jesus showed us how to battle back at deadly doubt: hold fast to the Word of God. Satan hates us enough to delight in our destruction, and Jesus knew better than to enter into a debate with Satan. Instead, Jesus spoke with authority by using the Word of the Father, steady in knowing God's Word is the irrefutable truth. To every temptation and invitation to doubt, Jesus said, "It is written, . . . it is written, . . . it is written. . . ."

This is how it is possible for us humans to battle back at doubt: by knowing and trusting God's Word. The need for spiritual security is one of our deepest human needs. Jesus shows us how to hold fast to God's words, which are always true—and he shows us what can happen when we do as he did in the desert: After Jesus said—not once but three times—"It is written," Matthew 4 tells us, "the devil left him."

Jesus said that if we hold to his teaching, we will know the truth and the truth will set us free (John 8:31–32).

Abortion has placed us in opposition to God's teachings and commands to love the Lord our God with all our heart, soul, mind, and strength—and to love our neighbors as ourselves (Luke 10:27). Instead we loved and worshiped the things of the world, or our own ideas, or our own security. We haven't loved others—not even ourselves.

Yet, when we chose abortion, our needs were real. Can we possibly trust God now without doubt—perhaps for the first time in our lives? Many voices have said we should not, and we need not—we have been encouraged to believe the lie that life is up to us and us alone.

Tasting the Truth

The failure of my marriage was a wake-up call that left me much more willing to listen to God. I didn't want any more spectacular failures in my life. After dropping out of college, experiencing a broken engagement, abortion, and now divorce, I knew I needed to find a new way of life—for the sake of my two children if not for myself. I continued to pursue my faith in the support group where I had met my Christian friend.

Then in 1991 I met the man who is now my husband, and we began attending church together. The Bible came alive for me, and I began to be able to discern between abortion rhetoric and the truth. I wanted to go beyond the slogans and the headlines and the protests and the hurt. I deeply needed to know what really happened, from God's point of view, as a result of my choice for abortion.

In the ensuing years, while doing a daily radio feature called *Life Redeemed*, I continued to learn as I interviewed pastors and Christian ministry leaders such as Gary Thomas, best-selling author of *Sacred Marriage* and several other books. Thomas pointed out something that you've probably already felt and feared; when you choose abortion, there is a spiritual deception:

> Abortion kills, steals, and destroys. If that sounds familiar, it should; because Jesus said in John 10:10 that Satan, the thief, comes to kill, to steal, and to destroy. If you want to know where abortion comes from, all you have to do is listen to the testimony of those who have experienced it. They're quoting Scripture and they don't even know it.[4]

These are words from someone whose ear is attuned to hear and speak God's truth.

Your ear for hearing truth improves as you open up your heart. There is no biblical record of the modern practice of abortion-on-demand in the Bible, but we don't have to settle for spiritual confusion and doubt as to whether it is a sin.[5] We can know for certain where God stands. As we get to know his nature in the Bible, the Holy Spirit teaches us about his wisdom regarding every trait of human nature (John 14:26).

For example, Internet pornography, sexting, and watching graphic sexual content in films are not mentioned in the Bible. Most of us know instinctively, however, that God doesn't endorse such actions that lead us away from him and toward our own ruin. So when we hear Jesus say that lust in our hearts is equal to lustful actions (Matt. 5:28), we understand we have begun to hear the truth. Next we may wonder how to meet God's impeccably high standards, especially since Jesus promises that God's law is perfect (Matt. 5:17–19). Through Jesus Christ and the Holy Spirit we may understand God's character, his intentions, and his ethics. Then our hearts may even begin to sense the wisdom and truth embedded in God's rules and regulations relating to how we are to regard and respect all human life.

Embracing the Truth

Abortion poses two serious problems for those who want to listen to God's voice and avoid sin. God says don't shed innocent blood, and God says do choose life.

Psalm 106 tells us how God's people strayed from him, stopped listening to him, and began to practice all kinds of wickedness and wrongdoing.[6] They listened to all the wrong voices—their own and others'—and began to worship false gods. Soon they were sacrificing children to these false gods. They shed innocent children's blood and it cost God's people, the Israelites, their homeland. They were distanced from God. This time in Israel's history illustrates how shedding children's innocent blood is a deep offense to God in violation of the prohibition against murder in Exodus 20:13.[7]

Murder is a harsh word—one I found so hard to accept after abortion. It helped to have a definition from the Scriptures. God defines those whose lives have been taken without provocation as having innocent blood, and he defends them by directing serious penalties and punishments against anyone doing such harm, using the word *murder* to mean *killing without God's permission* (Deut. 19:4–13).[8]

In the New Testament, Jesus said everyone violates the spirit of this law, and he identified murder as a spiritual heart problem rooted in angry thoughts that devalue others (Matt. 5:21–22).

Devaluing others through shedding innocent blood always carries a consequence in our hearts. Blood is God's copyright on life itself. He retained all rights to it when he gave humans our free will. He cannot overlook how it is spilled. Every child has his or her own blood, with separate DNA from his or her mother. This blood is present as the life force of each child from the very beginning—for all created beings "life . . . is in the blood" (Lev. 17:11). Every abortion sheds a child's innocent blood.

This can be shattering news to receive after the fact. Only the coldest heart chooses murder with eyes wide open. I believe we may only find courage to face the idea of God's judgment of abortion as prenatal murder by pursuing the love we have found in Jesus Christ. We were deceived and gave in to the temptation to fix our problem at any cost; we listened to the lies. Now, hearing and receiving the truth is the start of a new life with God (James 1:13–18). Our love relationship with God means we may now begin to order our lives around his truth. As we do, our ethics and morals will shift.

In short, we will be so heartbroken by abortion, we will listen to God when he says, "Choose life."

Accepting the Truth

God knows we are at times faced with gut-wrenching, irrevocable decisions. So he gave us instructions for how to choose in a life or death decision (Deut. 30:11–20). In essence he has said that we are without excuse on this matter because his commands are known to us—his desires are embedded in us, in our hearts, by his design. We are hardwired to choose life rather than abortion when we are given all the facts. For example, *The New England Journal of Medicine* reports women considering abortion feel loyalty, and are perhaps more likely to choose life, if given the chance to see an ultrasound image of the developing child.[9]

Even so, we tell ourselves that God cannot possibly have meant this difficult instruction for me in the midst of my impossible circumstances.

Listen to God anticipating our objections to his objectives:

> [To choose life over death] is not too difficult for you or beyond your reach. It is not up in heaven, so you have to ask, "Who will ascend into heaven to get it and proclaim it to us so we may obey it?" Nor is it beyond the sea. . . . No, the word is very near you; it is in your mouth and in your heart so you may obey it. (Deut. 30:11–14)

Choosing to take a life through abortion thus becomes much more than an expression of preference or the exercise of free will and practical wisdom. The choice to listen to God's voice and choose life becomes a moral act.[10] Will we listen to what God has said, or will we give in to the temptation to believe a lie or dismiss a difficult truth and try to be like God? When God explicitly commands what we are to choose, our choices reveal whether or not we agree God has the right to tell us how we are to choose. Will we give him our respect and the kind regard he says he wants from us? God promises to bless us for our love and worship of him, and he quickly warns we will destroy ourselves as a consequence of failing to be true to him. When we choose to listen with our hearts, we hear God explicitly instruct us, "Choose life, so that you and your children may live and that you may love the LORD your God" (Deut. 30:19–20).

God says there is an inextricable connection between choosing life, letting children live, and having a love relationship with God. God challenges us: *What did you actually put first, love most, or worship as you chose abortion?*

As I tried to put my life back together after abortion, I clearly put my hopes in my radio career to protect me and bring me honor, so I made it the source of all rewards in life. As time went on and I continued to hide from God and the truth of abortion, I began to believe in my work so deeply it almost equaled a kind of religious faith. In fact, my work had become the measure for the rest of my life. I put my reputation first, thinking if I cultivated a good name and matching image, that would make me good. You may do the same thing. If you love your lifestyle or status, you may define your worth by possessions or positions. Your actions, choice of friends, and home address become reflections of the high value you place on those things. Even good things can be subverted into other gods that you worship. Although you don't call it worship, that's exactly what it is when you yield your heart and will to those things. God wants you to seek him instead, and believe his promise for good things in return.

This is what Jesus was telling the woman at the well: God is our source. He cares most about our love relationship with him. Our world may value self-reliance and individual rights, but God says forsaking his living water to dig our own well is doubly sinful (Jer. 2:13). This is not the end of the story, however. We can begin to listen to God and begin a new life today. This is God's desire—that we return to him, determined to listen and to do what he says.

The way we answer the command to obey God always sums up how much we love him and worship him as God. Is it possible God views the choice for abortion, or not choosing life, as worshiping other gods?

Eve didn't physically bow down and worship Satan. All she did was allow him to cause her to doubt God's love. Then she was his.

Listening to the lies of abortion— *this is not a real person, not a baby, not a life*—sets us up to doubt the truth and then to choose death. Believing those lies makes it easier to doubt there will be consequences from trying to be like God, and that leads to more lies:

> *But what about my life? I didn't even know the guy.*
> *I was drunk at a party. Should this cost me my scholarship?*
> *Must I pay with the rest of my future for one indiscretion?*
> *I'm too young to be a mother and to give a child up would be too cruel.*

Whether you doubt God like Eve, or ignore and deny needing him as I did and the people of Israel did, after abortion, we must confront our choice. Although God put the truth within us, many of us chose to be deceived. Our wish to be free of the obligation of motherhood overrode our ability to discern the lies when others told us that what we were to abort was "just tissue" and "not a baby."

Later, in the emptiness of finding ourselves utterly and finally alone, or even in the light of truth dawning through a subsequent pregnancy and birth, we may hear ourselves muttering, "I didn't know. I didn't know." Even then, pride dies hard. We tell ourselves that somehow we are still in charge, and somehow none of this matters, as we try to carry on in life. We continue in our self-reliant doubt, without hope.

Now is the time to pause and recall again how Jesus sees us through eyes of love, and comes to help us move from the pain of the past to satisfy our thirst for love and relationship. As we begin to accept that we were deceived and that we listened to lies when we took that fatal action, a new temptation may seize us—the temptation to give up in despair. Fight back. Speak God's Word as Jesus did when the devil tempted him. Tell yourself the truth. Recall how Jesus said, "I am the way and the truth and the life" (John 14:6) and "Take heart! I have overcome the world" (16:33). Remind yourself that we know the outcome of this war—Jesus has defeated abortion's many sins by paying for it in full. We can say, "Thanks be to God, who gives us the victory through our Lord Jesus Christ" (1 Cor. 15:57 NASB). Listening to God's voice will help us withstand the temptation to condemn ourselves, and even when it's hard to believe, we will be left with peace.

The Bible says the enemy is the eternal accuser of those who have chosen to believe in Jesus Christ as our defense in the battle against sin—and we who believe have already overcome him by confessing that our only hope is in the blood Jesus shed in the battle for our souls (Rev. 12:10–11).

God did not leave Adam and Eve hopeless. Even as he was announcing the consequences for their sin, he provided "a whisper of hope uttered in the same breath as his initial judgment against evil."[11] God revealed his plan for the woman's offspring to crush the enemy of humankind (Gen. 3:15). Jesus is the fulfillment of this plan, and his early victory over temptation in that arid wilderness was only a foretaste of his ultimate defeat of all death on the cross and in his glorious resurrection.

Believing the truth activates God's plan for our future. This begins by accepting the verdict that abortion is a sin because it is a choice for death, a choice that sheds innocent blood. As we stand accused, we also stand forgiven. Abortion is grievously wrong, but abortion is not an unforgivable sin. Jesus died, and with his blood covering our sins, God's forgiveness is complete. He has cradled our most sinful hearts within his tender care.

—— *Reflect* ——

Read for yourself Genesis 2:4–3:24, the account of how the devil tempted Adam and Eve. Now notice in Matthew 4:1–11 the similar tactics employed in the temptation of Christ. This is the reality of how the devil works in this world. But read also in Galatians 5:16, the Holy Spirit overcomes the lust of the flesh as we walk by the Spirit. Where there is no revelation (God's message in the mind's eye) the people cast off restraint (easily violating God's law) according to Proverbs 29:18; but Jesus says to be encouraged because he has overcome everything in and of this world, including the devil and all of his tactics meant to undermine our trust in God, and there is no doubt about it according to John 16:33. As you think on his promise, also think upon these words from God:

- "Do not love the world or anything in the world. If anyone loves the world, the love of the Father is not in him. For everything in the world—the cravings of sinful man, the lust of his eyes and the boasting of what he has and does—comes not from the Father but from the world. The world and its desires pass away, but the man who does the will of God lives forever" (1 John 2:15–17).
- "'Then you will call upon me and come and pray to me, and I will listen to you. You will seek me and find me when you seek me with all your heart. I will be found by you,' declares the LORD, 'and will bring you back from captivity. I will gather you from all the nations and places where I have banished you,' declares the LORD, 'and will bring you back to the place from which I carried you into exile'" (Jer. 29:12–14).
- "Some people . . . think that we live by the standards of this world. For though we live in the world, we do not wage war as the world does. The weapons we fight with are not the weapons of the world. On the contrary, they have the divine power to demolish strongholds. We demolish arguments and every pretension that sets itself up against the knowledge of God, and we take captive every thought to make it obedient to Christ" (2 Cor. 10:2–5).
- "If you hold to my teaching, you are really my disciples. Then you will know the truth, and the truth will set you free" (John 8:31–32).
- "The reason the Son of God appeared was to destroy the devil's work" (1 John 3:8).

- "This is how you can recognize the Spirit of God: Every spirit that acknowledges that Jesus Christ has come in the flesh is from God, but every spirit that does not acknowledge Jesus is not from God" (1 John 4:2–3).

—— Request

Jesus, I praise you for completely overcoming Satan in the war of deception. Help me to be true to your Word and not doubt the truth about abortion or anything else you teach me by your Word and the Holy Spirit. I want to follow you, Lord. Help me to believe you will not leave me. Thank you for listening to my prayers. Help me listen to you as I read your Word, feel your nudges in my life, think on your will. Please help me obey what you say. I willingly give you all my love. In your name, I pray. Amen.

—— Respond

- If you haven't yet done so, recruit a prayer partner to meet with regularly. Ask God to help you identify a person who is able to keep a confidence and pray with you over the questions that arise as you study your Bible and learn new truths. If you sense God may want you to apologize for or have caring conversations about your abortion, discuss this possibility and seek God's direction in prayer.
- As a way to listen to God's love for children before their birth, set aside time to read Psalms 51 and 139, and Luke 1:39–42. As you read Psalm 51, write your reaction to the idea that a person can have a character trait from the time our mothers conceive us. Record your thoughts as you read in Psalm 139 how God knit you together in your mother's womb. Try to describe the significance of babies within their mothers' wombs responding to each other as described in Luke 1.
- Songs for hearing God's voice: The hymn "The Lord's Prayer" sets the words of Jesus in Matthew 6:9–13 to music to make this universally loved and effective prayer even more memorable. Also

"Speak O Lord" by Stuart Townsend and Keith Getty is a contemporary praise song that helps you come to the Lord to receive his comfort and truth, reminding us that our best weapon in a spiritual battle is Jesus and his Word.

Part Two

God's Heart

A Demonstration

Do you believe your heart can change?

After abortion, part of you is gone and you are not the same. You know something has been lost. You may feel like less of a person somehow, but you don't want others to know. An unnamed shame takes over. You want to withdraw, either to nurse the hurt to your wounded dignity or to avoid detection by those whose dignity appears intact.

The hard truth is that you cannot diminish the worth and personhood of a child before birth without diminishing the worth of your womanhood too. Like me, as a young woman you may have followed the feminist crowd, believing abortion would add to your value in the workplace as a woman unhindered by the responsibility of raising a child. "Reproductive freedom" was supposed to elevate the role of women in society to equal status with men who can choose to remain unencumbered by unwanted pregnancy or parenthood. Or you may have been stripped of your ability to protect your growing child if you were coerced into abortion as so many women are. Your partner or parents may have threatened to abandon you or expose you to public shame.

Whether by choice or by coercion, abortion always demeans your value as a woman, your identity as the vessel for God's creation of each new life. A woman's worth is not solely defined by childbearing, of course. But what sets us apart as women is our capacity to bear children.

Abortion strips us of the dignity of our unique role in producing human life, and wherever dignity has departed, shame resides.

Withdrawing does not heal the hurts.

Imagine a woman living in the shadow of an unnamed shame based not on abortion, nor on any sin, but rooted in a physical affliction beyond her control. This woman's desire to restore her body's dignity drove her to such desperation that she eventually came out of her seclusion to publicly reach out from among a crowd to seek help.

What if your reach for help could bring healing, new life, and a new identity all at once?

For one woman, it did. And her demonstration of faith, of reaching for healing to begin with, is what moved her healer to make a demonstration of his own. He demonstrated how much he loved her and what power he possessed to heal her and bring wholeness and dignity to both body and soul.

In Touch with Healing

Merry had grown up in a perfectly manicured place with perfectly manicured neighbors to match. Maintaining a perfect image seemed to be everything. But she wasn't perfect, and she needed a break. As a preteen she'd had the first of several accidents due to her monthly cycle, which arrived at irregular intervals with a heavy flow. It happens to young women every day, and even mature women can be caught off guard by it. But at such a young age, Merry's bleeding became a public joke. These minor mishaps might have been quickly forgotten in a less superficial environment, but in her perfect neighborhood the stories lived on, leaving her with the nickname "Bloody Merry."

The childhood recriminations followed Merry into adulthood, though she pursued a habit of keeping to herself. Feeling invisible was painful in a numb and quiet way, not like the heat of scorn when she was younger.

Endometriosis isn't contagious, she thought, recalling with shame an accidental stain noticeable when she stood up from the couch of someone she once visited. But the incident was like the proverbial final straw. She began to avoid people, as if she did carry some disease. Withdrawing just made more sense than risking further public ridicule.

Still, Merry knew God cared and she never gave up on seeking a cure. Her heart was so full of love she had never had the chance to share. All those years of longing for a normal life—she desperately wanted to find her place in the world. When she heard of a faith healer visiting her college campus, she knew she had to risk going to meet him, even though she was bleeding that day. This healer had gained quite a reputation across the country as he reached out to the blind, handicapped, and mentally ill. The official in town who summoned the healer was a man of faith, and hoped the healer could help his dying daughter.

People, hearing that the healer was on his way, emptied the classrooms, cafeteria, and dorms to get a glimpse of him. Despite the crush of people, her discomfort among so many unfamiliar faces, Merry joined the throng.

I've got to get close to him, she thought. *Maybe touching him could somehow help me too.*

She didn't realize until she was standing almost next to him that he was surrounded by bodyguards who were trying to keep people from getting too close. It was mayhem—shoulders, elbows, hips, and feet pressed in from every side. In part fear and part faith, she dropped to her knees. If she could only touch him, she believed, she could be healed. Desperate, she reached out for his clothing, which she somehow managed to brush with her fingertips at a hem. She was so stunned she hardly realized the silence settling, even as a voice echoed over the din.

All eyes were on the healer as he repeated, "Who touched me?"

Now the collective focus shifted from the man to . . .

Merry crouched lower, if that was possible, as the man's handlers argued over whether and how well they had protected him. With her face turned to the ground, she suddenly knew her bleeding had stopped. *Could it be so?* she wondered and began ever so slightly to straighten.

The man was insisting now, "Who touched me?" for he felt the power had gone out from him.

Merry froze. She knew he also knew. The power of merely his touch had healed her. There was no longer any reason to crawl! She stood tall and those around her watched the man fix his gaze on her.

Even as she stood before him, Merry felt her knees weaken. She fell at his feet, the story of the hard, long years of pain and isolation spilling out in blessed relief. The crowd no longer mattered as she heard herself tell him how his mercy, love, and grace had made her clean.

"Daughter," he said, as he cradled her chin in his hand, "your faith has made you well. Go enjoy the good life you have been given."

She smiled at the irony of it all. She had sunk so low, and yet the decision to crawl to his feet, to believe he would take her shame and give her dignity in return, take her sense of worthlessness and give her healing because she was worth everything to him, had lifted her to a new life of belonging to him in wholeness, love, and hope.

Reaching Out

What would you give if all the shame and worthlessness you feel after abortion could be relieved with just a touch? It can, though it's not a hem to reach for but a heart—Christ's heart. The Bible tells us that Jesus is the healer who demonstrates his love for us as a loving father cares for his own child. We have only to reach out, as Merry did, to receive that gift.

Just as Jesus knew, despite the crowd of people pressing in on him, that she desperately needed his life-changing power, he knows exactly what you need. There is a world clamoring for help and healing, but your specific needs, your hurts, are on Jesus' heart.

John says it this way: "How great is the love the Father has lavished on us, that we should be called children of God! And that is what we are! . . . Everyone who has this hope in him purifies himself, just as he is pure" (1 John 3:1, 3).

Do you believe Jesus is fully God and that he still has the power to heal? The bleeding woman's faith in Jesus changed her in God's eyes. His purity made her pure, and her purity made her his own child.

This is the basis for our hope of spiritual healing—the removal of shame and feelings of worthlessness—after abortion.

I'm struck by the truth of this dramatic change in the life of the bleeding woman who "had suffered a great deal under the care of many doctors, and had spent all she had, yet instead of getting better she grew worse" (Mark 5:26).

What an apt description for those of us who also have sought to relieve our wounded dignity after abortion. We've sought help, and sometimes put too much faith in all the deficient sources for complete healing.

False healing with counsel alone

Many of us have turned to the medical community and counselors to help our bleeding spirits, but instead found ourselves getting worse, suffering under the care of doctors.

Certainly, there are legitimate uses of psychiatry and psychology for mental and emotional problems. (See appendix A to connect with Christian counseling resources.) A skilled practitioner can teach good mental hygiene, pointing out flawed thinking and suggesting ways to keep your thought life healthy.

But when it comes to seeking counseling for depression and other emotional problems after abortion through the medical community, help can be hard to find. The Centers for Disease Control and Prevention (CDC), for example, warns of the dangers of postpartum depression after child loss saying, "[W]omen's reproductive experiences could be related to depression" following child loss due to miscarriage, stillbirth and infant death; and yet child loss due to abortion is not addressed in this same CDC resource.[1] And the American Psychological Association has gone on public record with their research findings, which effectively dismiss a need for mental health help after abortion.[2] For these reasons, many mental health professionals may remain unaware of the spiritual challenges so many of us face. And even the most sensitive and skillful mental health care counselor cannot help to heal a spiritual wound. Only God's truth can restore the bleeding heart and mind and soul.

I discovered this spiritual gap when, a few years after my abortion, on the advice of a friend, I sought counseling from a credentialed professional counselor. My friend saw how I struggled so with prolonged sadness over the abortion that resurfaced with each new emotional challenge in life. I was unable to resolve the pain of a divorce in my family and I went through strained romantic relationships, always battling feelings of low self-worth. It didn't take long for this practitioner to discern my problem was more than just managing emotions. What I needed to deal with was spiritual. At the root of all my shame and feeling of worthlessness, I felt alienated from God and feared I was going to hell for what I'd done when I chose abortion. I told her my concerns were based in my understanding of the teachings of my childhood Christian faith.

Instead of suggesting I connect with a church or a source related to my faith, she shared her belief in a watered-down version of eternity as infinite space. She encouraged me to believe that each of us, including my unborn child, has power over our own life and birth. She didn't bother to explain if this idea was rooted in another religion or her personal opinion, she simply stated that we each choose our own parents and determine when we will come into being. She added that my child had exercised personal power in choosing not to be born, returning to the cosmos to be born at a different, more beneficial time.

Even with my scant knowledge of God's promises and truth at that time, I was shocked. *A cosmic baby calling the shots? We each control how to be born and when and how to die?* This was not only unbiblical, but struck me as nonsensical.

Yet in desperation for relief, I continued to see this counselor, even allowing her to place her hands on my abdomen as she spoke an incantation about light and the child's spirit. That ungodly counseling experience was deeply unsatisfying and unhelpful, like what else ensued. She advised me to state to myself positive affirmations of my self-worth, rehearse my childhood hurts, and fix my mind on cosmic imagery, which totally sidestepped my real need. This blend of new age mysticism, wishful thinking, and what was called "healing" touch reflected a spirituality based on a false faith in things that cannot save and heal us, and were as prescriptive as a Band-Aid for the deep wounds of shame and guilt. That false faith could never fully address those wounds and answer the questions that lay at the root of my spiritual struggle after abortion: *Did my actions mean I was going to hell for having taken a life? How could I celebrate the idea of a child in heaven if I had forever forfeited my right to go there?*

Longing to know the truth about the hope of heaven and the reality of hell are universal needs, especially after an abortion brings you face to face with these questions. God, after all, has set eternity in our hearts (Eccl. 3:11). We need truth we can rely on when it comes to matters so infinitely great and so personally significant.

So as I continued to wrestle with these questions, I spent more money and time on other counselors who tried to help, but didn't go as far as the bogus healer who tried to break abortion's grip by speaking wishful words over my abdomen. These other practitioners listened as I confessed having an abortion and also shared new grief over the breakdown of my first marriage and the death of other family members. Still, they never addressed the root issue of all my grief—the abortion that was the root of my deeper distress with each new loss and trouble. These counselors also did not try to guide me into God's truth or help me find the spiritual help I needed.

I'm not dismissing the merits of counseling. It's possible to find a caring mental health professional who understands abortion as a spiritual crisis and who can direct you to the help you need from the church and other believers. Having someone to simply listen to your struggles and affirm sad feelings can be helpful, for instance. But without God's truth even the best talk therapy is not healing. There is a difference between *help* and *healing*, and broken hearts need God's *healing* touch. It's healing that will remove our guilt, bring us peace with God, and resolve the confusing grief over failing to prevent the death of a child.

False help as seen on TV

If I couldn't find relief as I turned to counselors for help, there were even fewer resources to be found in pop culture and media. The truth is, abortion is horrible, dark, and ugly. Children die. Women are hobbled spiritually as their God-given identity as mothers is denied. Men are stripped of their masculine dignity as fathers, protectors, and providers. But in the media and popular press you won't find those truths, or any real relief for the troubling spiritual questions abortion raises as you search in books, movies, or magazines, on radio, television, or the Internet. The network news seldom portrays abortion as detrimental, or even as a wrong or mistaken action. The question of the eternal fate of the child is replaced by the idea that you simply made a choice, and there never was a child involved at all. This can actually increase your shame, leaving you feeling worse and thinking, *Why am I still so distressed?*

Anne said, "After my two abortions, whenever the media portrayed abortion as just a woman's right to choose, I would feel as if I was choking on the weight of my choice. Nobody ever mentioned the cost of that choice—the death of a living human child, my child." The talk shows and daytime television aimed at empowering women and increasing self-esteem from a feminist viewpoint are meant to make you feel better, not lead you into truth.

On the other hand, God never suggests you can overcome pain by trying to minimize the impact of what you've done. He isn't about suggesting a remedy for the heartaches of abortion. Rather, God promises to "heal the brokenhearted" through the sacrificial love of Jesus (Isaiah 61:1 NKJV).

Anne learned that true emotional peace had to be founded on something more than feeling good about her choices. She says, "Only through my faith in Jesus have I found a way to satisfy my hunger to know how God regarded both me and my children after I made that choice."

False hope from the self-help shelf

In the ten years immediately following my abortion, I lived my life apart from God, placing my faith in the self-help movement. I was willing to try anything if I thought it would bring me peace. So I spent more money and time on books about how to live and take care of emotional wounds. I became an armchair expert on relationships and coping. I became a burbling fountain of unsolicited advice. I was one of those women who gobbled pop psychology like candy, looking for a quick fix to relieve my pain and guilt.

It's no coincidence magazines full of such junk advice are also full of gossip. Just like celebrity hounds, we keep chasing whatever we think will give us something dressed up as good, right, appealing, and attractive in our own eyes. We keep trying to get close to the source of some healing. But none of it has the power to change us, because none of it is based in truth.

When such false faith fails, you can once again blame yourself, but that just makes your sense of shame and worthlessness worse.

The Bible says it isn't even possible to help yourself. It's not a remedy that's needed. You need a redeemer, because you and I are powerless over sin—sin makes each one of us worthless (Rom. 3:9–20). Seeking worldly answers in desperate self-reliance is an exercise in futility that can never heal the wounded heart.

My quest for self-help was no different from the woman who had been bleeding for twelve years. And just like Merry, I remained in a sort of spiritual quarantine, spending all my time and money on help for a condition I could not control, when what I really needed was God's mercy and grace.

Jesus Heals the Wounded Heart

Jesus will not shun nor shame us over our spiritual agony after an abortion. Jesus had compassion on the crowds who followed him in need of healing (Matt. 14:14). He sees us as harassed and helpless when we are without his spiritual leadership in life (Matt. 9:35–36). He knows we cannot save ourselves. Instead, he will exercise his power to take on the sin and shame, heal our affliction, and give us a new status as children of God because of his love. We have only to open our hands and hearts to receive this gift. Do we want it? Are we willing to reach out for it?

How easy it would have been for the bleeding woman in Mark 5:24–34 to answer *no*. The risk seems *too much*, the gap between her shame over her chronic unclean state and the perfect healer *too far*, the courage to reach through the crowd *too exhausting*. But hope propelled her as she reached out to him for what the world had withheld from her for so long.

Jesus realized healing power had gone out from him before he even turned and asked, "Who touched me?"

What an intriguing question from Jesus, who knows everything that ever was or will be. He knows a secret act of faith, just as he knows our secret acts of sin.[3] But he doesn't desire for our faith to reside in the shadows. His insistence gave her the courage she needed to fall at his feet and tell him the whole truth. His question wasn't an accusation, but a chance for her to declare her faith—so Jesus could then demonstrate his claim for her as his own. Because as far as Jesus is concerned, our faith is at the heart of the matter whenever we need healing.

That is what Jesus' question was all about—he didn't ask because he needed to know, but because the people around him did. He was demonstrating the connection between healing and faith in that crowd, and in ensuing encounters too—when he responded to a direct request for healing from a blind man, and to another who was mute. He asked each person a clarifying question about their faith. When each affirmed a belief in Jesus' ability to heal them, he said, "According to your faith will it be done to you" (Matt. 9:27–30). And so it was. For these two men, and for the bleeding woman, it was faith, after all, that brought about the healing.

And it is our faith in him that brings us into this close family relationship where the love of Jesus heals us. As the Bible says in John 1:12–13, "To all who received him, to those who believed in his name, he gave the right to become children of God—children born not of natural descent, nor of human decision or a husband's will, but born of God."

After abortion the spiritual afflictions of shame and feeling brokenhearted can be healed completely according to our faith.

Risking All

Paula learned this. She felt ashamed after her husband coerced her into an abortion with threats of violence. Afterward, there seemed nowhere to turn. Her abusive marriage grew even more so, as her husband threatened to tell all their family and friends about the abortion unless she did as he said.

"People assume it's your fault if you're poor, and if your husband is violent," she explains. "I knew abortion was wrong, but I pictured myself trying to feed our already hungry kids with no heat, no warm clothes. When he threatened me, it all became simply overwhelming. After the abortion, [when] he threatened to expose me, I never felt so trapped."

Paula lost all faith—in herself and in God. She felt devalued by her husband's abuse, and the more abusive he became, the less she was worth in her own eyes. She even began to blame herself for failing to find a solution to their poverty, the fact that another child was on the way, and then the abortion itself that she felt pressured to get.

She could have been just another statistic, the one that says the risk of violence and homicide from their partners is a real danger to pregnant women.[4] But her parents never stopped demonstrating their love for her and sharing God's love for her.

When Paula began to believe in that love, she shared the secret of what was happening in her home. Her parents grieved with her, both over the abuse and for the lost child and grandchild. They looked for ways to help her and provided crucial support during a dangerous time. (See appendix A for resources, and seek help immediately if you are subject to threats of violence or abuse that leave you feeling vulnerable or unsafe.) The caring support of her family enabled Paula to see herself as worthy of love and respect, increasing her faith and trust in God to heal her of the hurts of abortion and abuse. "By reaching out for the love I had always needed, I found what had always been there for me to receive," she says. Faith is what got her through those dark days and faith is what helped her reach out for help and healing. If you have been devalued through abuse or other suffering, it can be difficult to reach out in hopes of getting the help you need—but if we never risk reaching out to people, we may never feel the full measure of God's grace to change our lives.

In Touch with Truth

That kind of faith heals not only your heart but also impacts the hearts of all those around you by demonstrating God's power to make us new. The bleeding woman in Mark 5 was considered unclean and impure by those around her.[5] In that day, when a Jewish man's clothes came in contact with a bleeding woman's clothes, he would have had to leave the crowd to pursue a ritual cleansing. Instead, Jesus completely redefined God's standards (Lev. 15:19–31) in order to make her clean. Jesus rewrote the rules on purity and righteousness through one suffering woman who dared to put her hope in him.

He asked, "Who touched me?" not to expose her to shame but to allow her to show the crowd a stunning new definition of righteousness and healing.

The implications for us who suffer after abortion are equally stunning. God no longer counts any sin, our own or anyone else's, against us because of our faith in Jesus and his sacrifice. Jesus doesn't just remedy our sin. He takes it. He removes it and he makes us pure, clean, and new. He did this for the bleeding woman in the most public way, by taking the private source of her personal shame in the midst of a crowd and letting the people know that the covering of his loving grace had completely healed her.

"God made him who had no sin to be sin for us," the Bible tells us, "so that in him we might become the righteousness of God" (2 Cor. 5:21). Jesus became our sin so we could be cleansed of it.

He makes you clean. He makes you new. He makes you pure.

Isn't that an amazing promise? "In Christ" you become a "new creation," like children, all new—not just cleansed, but no longer in any debt to God over sins (2 Cor. 5:17–19). You no longer need to withdraw or be ashamed or agonize.

TIMELESS TRUTH
Jesus heals us in order to make us his own children.

With that simple question, "Who touched me?" Jesus demonstrated that faith in him is all we need to be healed. He takes pure holiness wherever he goes and it flows out to all who reach out to him in faith. Think of this as purity by association. No matter what you have or haven't done, your faith means his righteousness actually becomes yours.

Having his purity not only restores but also elevates us, as we gain a new status in the family of God. The bleeding woman is the only woman Jesus called "Daughter" in all of Scripture. Granting her this status was of great significance—revealing the higher purpose for which she was healed. No earthly healing can accomplish all of that. But reaching out to Jesus in faith can make us his own dear children too. Jesus heals us in order to make us his own.

The healing of the bleeding woman was an interruption of Jesus' ministry appointment with the father of a dying girl who was desperate for Jesus' help. Jesus provided it, raising that man's daughter from the dead, and at the same time, he let everyone know that he had a daughter too—one he had given new life even before her death. One he cared about as much as any earthly father cares about a daughter who is afflicted and in need. Her brush with his healing power freed her from all suffering and need.

Of course that kind of faith, that new life, can take time for us to find. Thanks to a friend who helped me see God's love, after ten years of wandering in the world's values, I encountered the blessed relief of knowing Jesus had died to forgive me of all sin. God was not committed to punishing me as I deserved, but rather, Jesus had come to make a way for me to have peace with God. Other friends invited me to church and soon I was reading the Bible and studying the basics of Christian belief. My faith journey continued to unfold over another ten years of attending church and hearing God's Word rightly applied to the question of when life begins.

As my pastor preached from the Psalms, Isaiah, Jeremiah, and the Gospels, again and again I heard how our earthly lives begin when God decides to bring us into being. This knowledge was at times excruciating as I realized that when I chose abortion, I had not just ended a pregnancy but a life.

The agony of that knowledge was not something a counselor could talk away, and following the wisdom of the world was cold comfort when my need to grieve was never acknowledged. I needed Christ to take my agony and bind my bleeding heart and make it new.

Instead, I spent many long years seeking help in all the wrong places, and I avoided the church and spiritual community out of ignorance and fear.

This only added to my isolation and shame.

Yet Christ's love would not let me go, even as I hurt myself greatly with self-recrimination and self-rejection due to ignorant misunderstanding of God's purposes and plans. As a Christian with limited knowledge of God's healing grace, I renounced myself instead of my mistake, which only blocked my spiritual growth in faith. Feeling like an outcast in God's kingdom, I did what I could to try to fit in. My shame was still there, only now hidden behind a new mask of righteous perfection and piety. I proved to myself many times and in many ways, both outside church and as a new believer, that avoiding spiritual pain only prolongs it.

And this prolonging also served as a cushion from a pain more poignant and penetrating: my child was no more. Once I arrived at that conclusion, my emotions would at times feel overwhelming. Sudden waves of tears would appear while I was in worship, especially when called to a time of silent confession and prayer. I would have to hide my face in my hands so others wouldn't be alarmed by my loss of control. I couldn't give voice to the heartbreak I experienced, and yet I didn't wish to be consoled.

But, we can take heart that there will come a day when it will be possible to restrain these powerful emotions, a day when we will be lifted out of our pain, our losses, and our shame. As God's love has allowed us to see ourselves as Jesus sees us, we can also reach out to him, trusting his powerful love to change us and make us, and our children lost to abortion, his very own.

Jesus says, "Come to me, all you who are weary and burdened, and I will give you rest" (Matt. 11:28). When we reach out in faith, he cradles our hearts by his powerful ability to carry all our cares. He fulfills his promise to help us rest our weary souls as we turn every problem into prayers, especially prayers of praise for his amazing love.

I can remember quite clearly standing at the crossroads you now face with only my faith to carry me forward. I continued to look to Jesus, study his Word, pray for him to change my heart, believe. I learned that

Jesus' grace to save me is a gift (Eph. 2:8–9). Perhaps my hope of heaven was not in vain. Perhaps I really could overcome all this pain. Did I really believe that Jesus had a place for me with him, safe, protected, under his wings? Could he really love me so?

As I began to understand God's plan to restore the whole earth from the curse of sin and death, I found these words from Ecclesiastes 3:11: "[God] has made everything beautiful in its time."

I clung to that promise in pure faith, not knowing or seeing how in the world God could make my act of destruction beautiful. But I believed him. I became determined to learn about him and his ways until I could see how he would make his beauty true in my life, even in taking the life of my child through abortion.

He has done what he promised. I no longer feel the need to hide my heart (or a face full of tears) when I am around others who know the truth. I now have new desires to use my gifts and my time to help others instead of always striving through my career to prove my worth. I love my children exactly as they are, and value the precious gift of life each one represents. And I know the truth about the promise of heaven that I sought so desperately for years: the one who believes has eternal life.

When Jesus spoke of healing the lame man at the pool to the religious crowd who opposed him, Jesus said, "I tell you the truth, whoever hears my word and believes him who sent me has eternal life and will not be condemned" (John 5:24). And Jesus reassured one thirsty bedraggled woman from the wrong (Samaritan) crowd that drinking deep of his love wells up in us unto eternal life (John 4:14). By faith, a righteous yet lonely hurting woman became God's beloved child. And by faith we gain eternal life, given by Jesus and guaranteed by him in John 10:28–29 to all who share her faith in his power to heal our hearts.

I'm completely confident as you seek him, you too will see his beauty in your circumstances, no matter how ashen they seem. You will no longer feel you have to withdraw in shame, retreat from the world in worthlessness.

Once you have reached for and received the love of Jesus, the crowd no longer matters. The love of Jesus Christ moves you from the crowd to a cloud of eternal witnesses to the power and glory of God (Heb. 12:1).

God's acceptance purifies you for your place as one of his daughters in the forever family of God. Your healing becomes complete, and he remains ever faithful.

—— *Reflect* ————————————————————————

Read for yourself in Matthew 9, Mark 5, and Luke 8, the accounts of the bleeding woman. Note how the story is told as a companion story to that of Jesus healing the daughter of a righteous man. Pay special attention to the crowd's reactions. How would you respond if you heard Jesus was arriving at your church today? Would you reach out to him or shrink back for fear of disapproval? Are you a member of a group of believers in Jesus Christ as Lord? If not, what would have to change in order for you to feel safe to seek a community of Christ-followers? If our parents or other loved ones have been abusive or neglectful, the idea of dependence may call to mind a feeling of unsafe neediness or vulnerability. For a new definition of the idea of faith as dependence on God, read the following verses aloud and choose one to memorize this week:

- "[The Lord] heals the brokenhearted and binds up their wounds. He determines the number of the stars and calls them each by name. Great is our Lord and mighty in power; his understanding has no limit. The LORD sustains the humble but casts the wicked to the ground" (Ps. 147:3–6).
- "They will be called oaks of righteousness, a planting of the LORD for the display of his splendor" (Isa. 61:3).
- "He will not crush the weakest reed or put out a flickering candle. Finally he will cause justice to be victorious" (Matt. 12:20 NLT).
- "Having loved his own who were in the world, he now showed them the full extent of his love. . . . He . . . began to wash his disciples' feet" (John 13:1, 5).
- "Those who are led by the Spirit of God are sons of God. For you did not receive a spirit that makes you a slave again to fear, but you received the Spirit of sonship. And by him we cry, 'Abba, Father.' The Spirit himself testifies with our spirit that we are

God's children. Now if we are children, then we are heirs—heirs of God and co-heirs with Christ, if indeed we share in his sufferings in order that we may also share in his glory" (Rom. 8:14–17).

—— *Request* ————————————————————

Lord, you have promised you will not reject anyone who comes to you. And you say when we believe in your power to heal us, then we are welcomed into your family as your very own children. It can seem too good to be true—this love that you have for us. Help us to be bold to come out of our isolation and fear of people and to believe in the power of your love to save us and purify us. I pray these things in your name. Amen.

—— *Respond* ————————————————————

- Worship God with a letter you write to him—a love letter telling him your heart. If you need help to structure your thoughts, try using the ACTS method of communicating and prayer:

  Adore God by praising his character, his holiness, the things about him that make him utterly worthy above all created life.

  Confess the things you've done and left undone that fall short of returning the love God has shown you.

  Thank God for all his benefits—things you otherwise take for granted that you know can only come from God.

  In **S**upplication, with a humble and dependent heart, ask God to grant your requests.

- Take a step of faith this week by joining a Bible-centered, grace-filled church where you can be baptized, or your dormant baptismal faith may be renewed. Visit a church or churches as you pray and discern where God would have you join the body of Christ. The Bible says it is as you reach out to receive his body and blood, you are healed (Matt. 26:26–28 and John 6:47–58). Take with you an open mind and an open heart and risk reaching out to meet new people and make new friends in church, taking as much time and as much care as you need to build relationships with others who are Christ-centered, spiritually healthy, and mutually respectful.

- Consider connecting to a church through your existing friendships and relationships with other people of faith. If someone has invited you in the past, or friends model faith you admire, ask to join them this week as they attend church.
- Songs of heaven and God's saving grace inspire and give us hope. James Rowe's classic hymn "Love Lifted Me" contrasts sinking deep in sin and being lifted to safety by God's love. "We All Bow Down" by Lenny Leblanc depicts people from all walks of life, the whole crowd of humanity, bowing and kneeling at Jesus' heavenly throne of grace. "Beautiful Things" by Gungor reinforces God's work to "make beautiful things out of dust." Listen to or sing these songs to yourself this week as your prayer to God. Watch how this prayer will buoy your spirit and connect you even more intimately to Christ's love for you.

A Realization

Can you believe this forgiveness?

It's a journey to find forgiveness for the past. The realization that the slate of all you've done can be wiped clean takes time, and an encounter with Christ. It's hard to believe that he will make your life new when you're so used to walking around in your shame, in your own self-condemnation.

What keeps you from believing that God does not withhold forgiveness or salvation from those who love him and who obey him? What keeps you from knowing Christ's cloak of salvation secures your place with him and covers all shame?

Is it enough just to know this truth?

No, you must come to experience it to find the blessed relief that you need not live in isolation forever from God. In fact, the Bible says, "Come near to God and he will come near to you" (James 4:8).

For me, that took time. I had to grow in faith to see some of my spiritual difficulties begin to recede. Though I wanted spiritual healing and turned to God for help, Jesus Christ had not yet become the goal of my faith. A crisis of seeing his love acted out for me forced a crucial question. *What about him?*

Abortion wounds our hearts—hardening us to the truth, or breaking us in sorrow and pain. Sometimes we experience both in an endless loop. Yet, Jesus awakens the cold and numb through his mercy, and comforts the sad and lonely by his grace—even those who think they have done the unpardonable.

The Convicted Heart

Concrete block walls threatened to echo whatever sound escaped a man's throat. Cold tile flooring promised to be easily wiped clean of his memory. No one would choose a room like this one as a place to die. Interior windows simultaneously separated and welcomed the spectators—officially known as "witnesses."

"We don't allow spectators!" The warden pointedly reminded his crew of their purpose, as he overheard the guards that milled around.

Yeah, right, the guard thought. *Witnesses, watching a spectacle, whether we want to be here or not.*

The state required a certain number of guards to be on duty for executions and his number was up, he joked to his buddies on the force. They stood in the back row, exchanging banter to break up the time.

"Hang in there," one said.

Gallows humor. Anyone in the trenches knew how to check out mentally in order to get through the gruesome parts of this job.

Surveying the crowd, the guard saw all the players in their places. Up front was the governor who ordered this shindig. *What an opportunist,* he thought. *Just trying to protect his turf.*

"Please, listen to me," the governor's wife beseeched the governor to give a last-minute reprieve.

The guard wondered if he could agree. No one seemed to be able to say what this guy had done to earn a death sentence. But plenty of people sure wanted him dead. *Where there's smoke, there's fire, right? What's it to me anyway?*

The guard looked around. The condemned man's family was here, but many a guilty man has gone to his death with faithful family standing close by. *This is no different,* he thought. *Their faces are always etched with pain.*

And yet something was different. This crowd around the condemned man was larger and all over the map, with angry people jeering over here and another group over there quietly weeping.

Who really knows if this guy is guilty and deserves to die? the guard thought. *Well, it's none of my business. I'm just following orders, and I have problems of my own. I need to just do this. I need the overtime.*

He looked up as the condemned man was led in, already battered and bloody.

"Man, why shake down a guy that hard when you're about to take him out?" he whispered to his buddy.

His colleague smirked. "I guess that's why those guys make the big cake."

The guard and his buddy were low-level civil servants. Their job was to ensure there wouldn't be any surprises and that the prisoner would "cooperate," as they were told, with the sentence. A lot of doomed men had to be dragged into this room kicking and screaming. He checked the time, relieved that he'd be out of there soon.

As much as he tried to hurry home in his mind, he was drawn in to the gaze of that gentle face dripping blood from the pre-execution rough-up. He had never seen eyes like that. There was no fight in the prisoner, but there was also zero fear. *Was that . . . courage?* People had often remarked that you had to be brave to be a prison guard, always exposed to danger from criminals in a dirty job like this, but at that moment he felt small and mean and even a bit ashamed.

When the warden asked if there were any last words, the condemned man seemed to recede from the scene. He gazed around the room. He wasn't speaking to anyone present and yet he seemed to be speaking to everyone when he said, "Forgive them, they don't know what they do."

Suddenly the guard knew this man did not deserve to die! He didn't know how he knew; he just knew the man was innocent. More than that, he knew that he himself was loved by this most innocent, gentle man.

He was forever changed by that gaze. Suddenly he found himself wishing the governor would bring this farce to a halt—that the infamous black phone would ring with a last-minute reprieve from some higher authority somewhere. Something, anything to stop what was about to occur.

But the execution went forward.

He could have sworn there was an earthquake at the man's last breath. It was an utterly dark moment—even in that dark place—which left him so shaken that he could seldom speak to others about all that he had seen and experienced that day.

Except to say, "I can't explain it, but somehow on that day, I felt like I looked into the face of God."

Mercy Received

Abortion leaves us sensing we have witnessed an execution. It leaves us wondering if we can ever be forgiven for it. It leaves us, at some point, facing God for the ways we have reacted to being part of the event. In that way, everyone is like the guards or the crowd, like the indifferent or the weeping or the angry around the death of Jesus, as recorded in Luke 23:13–49. We are all called to witness his execution.

Maybe you feel like the guards, not causing this man's condemnation, but asked to participate in the execution. Or maybe you feel like the weeping crowd, sad and remorseful. Or maybe you are among the angry, defensive crowd. Or maybe you are like the governor, Pilate, just trying to stay out of the fallout of some fight over God and religion. Or, like Pilate's wife, maybe you somehow knew truth but had no faith foundation on which to stand. Maybe you are like the religious leaders, relying on tradition and training. The disciples, the once-faithful, were scattered and silenced—fear blocks truth every time. A few devoted loved ones walked those horrible steps with him to Calvary, suffering and sharing his pain. And at the center of it all, we encounter Jesus.

So who best represents you? Where do you place yourself in the story?

I asked myself these questions when I attended a retreat where I experienced these events as a dramatic play. As the action unfolded on the stage, I found myself more and more outraged at the treatment Jesus received. At the time, I had believed in Jesus as my Savior for more than ten years, but I still worried over whether I had damned a baby to an eternal life in hell. I spent years silently begging God to forgive me. But never feeling forgiven, I decided to just forget. Weeping always returned, and I couldn't understand why.

Perhaps you too have tried to hide your true thoughts and feelings behind a mask of perfection. Fearing rejection, you try to earn favor and approval from others and even God, never sensing you're worthy of his love.

These patterns set the stage for my choice for abortion, and that terrible secret remained in my life, even with new friends in church. I allowed that secret to become a wall that kept guard on an area of my heart yearning for forgiveness. It was like that part of my heart, the part that could be completely exposed, was off-limits, even to myself.

Then on that retreat I asked myself who represented me, these guards who had only their own interests in mind as they carried on business as usual, or Christ himself who went to the cross to save my soul?

I watched as in the play the guards gambled for Jesus' clothes. I thought on the scriptural account: "When they came to the place called the Skull, there they crucified him, along with the criminals—one on his right, the other on his left. Jesus said, 'Father, forgive them, for they do not know what they are doing.' And they divided up his clothes by casting lots" (Luke 23:33–34).

And, "When the soldiers crucified Jesus, they took his clothes, dividing them into four shares, one for each of them, with the undergarment remaining. This garment was seamless, woven in one piece from top to bottom. 'Let's not tear it,' they said to one another. 'Let's decide by lot who will get it.' This happened that the scripture might be fulfilled which said, 'They divided my garments among them and cast lots for my clothing.' So this is what the soldiers did" (John 19:23–24).

I remembered reading in some study notes on the accounts that the law of the land at that time dictated that any possessions an executed person had with him could be taken by the executioners.[1] This was their right.

Then I watched the most excruciating part of the drama: the nails being driven into the hands and feet of Jesus, who died to save me.

When he said, "Father, forgive them, for they do not know what they are doing," it was as if my eyes, though wanting to shut out this agonizing scene, had been opened—because as Christ said this, the guards were dividing up the spoils, without a thought or a care of how he was suffering on their behalf. And by the conviction of the Holy Spirit, I saw I was no better than they. They were more concerned about exercising their rights than in the sacrifice Jesus was making out of love and grace and with forgiveness. In that moment I wondered, *Did I care how far Jesus had gone to save me?* Or was I simply relieved to have escaped the punishment I knew that I deserved?

I had to admit my heart had cared little for what it cost Jesus to free me from destruction. For the first time, I encountered his suffering, as he loved and prayed for those who were persecuting him. It became too horrible to bear. I did not want to be the cause of it, especially for one so beautiful and so brave. Even if it meant that I would have to die, I was willing to pay the price so Jesus would not have to endure such torture for me.

When the play was finished, Jesus' lifeless body was removed from the cross, and the sanctuary lights went dim. Silence settled in, save for a solo voice singing a refrain based on Jesus' words in Matthew 25:40. *Whatsoever you do to the least of my children, that you do unto me; whatsoever you do to the least of my children, that you do unto me.*

As one who felt compelled and called to come, I got up out of my seat and went forward to the altar. There I fell to my knees, with my heart sobbing, "I understand! I'm so sorry. Jesus, I've crucified you. I'm so sorry."

It was the moment I had been dreading and avoiding for as long as I could remember. I was face to face with God with my whole heart exposed, admitting exactly who I was—my pride crowning him with wounding thorns, my selfishness piercing his side. I cannot explain my honesty before God, except to say Jesus' courage made me brave to await the sentence I knew that I deserved.

But instead of punishing me, God gave me an astonishing answer— one completely unrelated to my guilty conscience. With kindness and care Jesus spoke into my heart a simple and direct instruction, *Tell them I love them.*

I was kneeling at Jesus' feet, feeling his heart beat for mine, and so surprised by this directive that my weeping suddenly ceased. I began to sense a new purpose—to love him and defend him and give him the honor he is due. And I began right away by praying, "But, Lord, I have crucified you."

I sensed him say, with infinite kindness and patience, *Now you understand.* And again, *Tell them I love them.*

I lingered there in prayer for the longest time with a calm and peace I had never known. When I finished, for the first time in my life, I felt worthy. I knew I was worthy because Jesus Christ had said so on the cross. He had a purpose for me that had nothing to do with all my fears and failures. It was all about him. All he wanted was for me to get beyond myself to open my eyes to what he had already done because of his great love. Jesus on the cross finally appeared real to me, I saw him for who he truly is. And I understood at last how much he has done to prove what he says my life is worth.

What he's done for me, he's done for you: you are worthy because he suffered and died for you there. And what he's said to me, he's saying to you: *I love you. Your sins are forgiven.*

"It is finished" (John 19:30).

Are You Ready?

There is no formula for how you encounter God's love. For me, meeting Jesus was at a retreat, in the middle of a passion play. For you, it may be at home or in the grocery store, or in a conversation with a friend or as you read something or hear a particular song. Jesus comes to meet us in so many ways, and his mission is always to restore our hearts for healthy relationships with God, ourselves, and others.

But are you ready to receive him? Are you ready to take the forgiveness he offers and forgive yourself?

Jeannie didn't know. She had been in relationships with two different men, each who forced her to choose abortion. Each man then later married other women with whom they started a family. The pain of this for Jeannie seemed too much to bear. The emotional wounds went deep, the feelings of rejection and sense of unworthiness.

"Why doesn't anyone want my babies?" she cried. The question drove her into a self-destructive lifestyle and made it difficult for her to believe in any kind of love, even love enough to forgive and free herself for a healthy, whole life.

That is what can happen, therapist Dr. Theresa Burke says. "Women will put themselves in precarious relationships and bad situations and sometimes abusive situations. Sometimes women will think, *there's nothing good ahead for me,* and this is where we really see the spiraling down."[2] Promiscuity, eating disorders, addictive behaviors, feelings of suicide—these are the things that can be triggered or worsened by abortion.[3] (See the listings in appendix A to find immediate help if you are troubled by feelings of suicide or emotional despair, or to find help with addictions and other life-controlling issues.)

Without feeling forgiven and forgiving oneself, you're never free from an enslavement to the sense of unworthiness that abortion can bring.

Jeannie discovered this when she entered a residential treatment program that introduced her to a greater love, support, and a family of faith for the first time in her life. She learned God doesn't reject you even if you fail to show him love. He wants you as part of his family. He loves you with a never-ending love. The blood he shed for you means you are eternally redeemed—bought back from your former way of life as one who is now set free (Heb. 9:14). Your ongoing sorrow does not mean he hates you, even if you have been indifferent to him in the past. He comes to clear the guilty conscience so we can draw near to Jesus, where he can cleanse and cradle our hearts.

Those truths brought new life to Jeannie, along with faith that God had not doomed her to a life without love. No, he loved her so much that he showed the world she meant everything to him, and he did it all from the cross.

Redeeming Love

That kind of love is so difficult to grasp. It's so divine, so unconditional and self-sacrificing that it hardly seems human.

The lack of loving relationships can be part of the problem leading to abortion to begin with, according to those who study the issue. Researcher Philip Ney says if you have been dehumanized through abuse or neglect, you will more likely be able to dehumanize your child and choose to abort.[4] Poor relationship patterns and the choice for abortion go hand in hand, as our character flaws often flow both to and from the choice to abort our child.

But encountering the merciful forgiveness of Jesus Christ in his death heals all wounded characters. When you are forgiven, you become free to forgive and build healthy relationships and love others in his name.

That is what happened to some of the guards and soldiers who witnessed Jesus' suffering on the cross. The Scriptures tell us how even they were changed: "When the centurion and those with him who were guarding Jesus saw the earthquake and all that had happened, they were terrified, and exclaimed, 'Surely he was the Son of God!'" (Matt. 27:54).

That centurion was a commander of one hundred men in the Roman army who oversaw the cruel mockery and torture of Jesus' crown of thorns. He led the hundreds who had been instruments in carrying out Jesus' death sentence. And he, too, was pierced with the truth that the blameless Christ loved even him enough to die for him. For him, the moment that truth struck his heart came with Jesus' loud cry, one markedly different from others he must have heard on the job in carrying out crucifixions for the Romans. For "the strength of his cry indicates that Jesus did not die an ordinary death of those crucified, who normally suffered long periods of complete agony, exhaustion, and then unconsciousness before dying."[5] No, what the centurion heard was a cry of divine love, of divine forgiveness.

For when Jesus died, the centurion "praised God" (Luke 23:47).

The Bible says in Romans 10:9, "If you confess with your mouth, 'Jesus is Lord,' and believe in your heart that God raised him from the dead, you will be saved."

Even the ones who made the horrible mistake of heartlessly crucifying Jesus found forgiveness when they confessed he is Lord, the Son of God.

What makes you or I think we deserve anything less?

Everyone who calls on his name will be saved (Rom. 10:13). This is the mercy of Jesus Christ on the cross.

His love does not depend on our treatment of him. He loved even the ones who nailed his hands and feet, who raised his cross, who divided up his clothes as he writhed naked and in pain. He loves you and me too. Though the Roman soldiers ignored and tortured him, he still loved them and prayed for them. Even more, he prayed that God would forgive them. His love and prayers changed their hearts.

Feeling the full weight and burden of abortion, can you fathom such love and forgiveness? Despite what you may have believed about God's wish to destroy you over all the wrong and pain of abortion, Jesus loves you. He always has. Even though you have done, or continue to do, things that grieve him, he loves you still. There is nothing you can do to earn his love for you, and nothing you can do to destroy his love for you. Think on that for a moment and let it astonish your heart: Jesus did not withhold his love and mercy to anyone as he faced death, even those who abused him without cause.

TIMELESS TRUTH
Jesus died to forgive all sin, even those sins that were yet to come.

Made New

That weekend I was at the retreat where this truth astonished my own heart, God was renewing me. First he pierced my heart, just as Jesus' side had been pierced on the cross, and all my own self-condemnation came spilling out. I began to open myself to the idea that he loved me no matter what.

Between retreat activities, I felt the Holy Spirit prompt me to be open and ready to receive, instead of keeping my usual reserve. So I struck up a conversation with a woman named Sandy. I was just trying to be friendly and make small talk when I asked Sandy to tell me about her family.

She replied that she had a son away at college, and she filled in a few details of his life. Then she paused and said, "But I also did a bad thing. I killed a child by abortion five years ago."

Without stopping to think, I revealed my secret. "So did I. Twenty-three years ago."

A woman named Jill overheard us. "My daughter had an abortion not long ago and she is so sad," Jill said. "I don't know how to help her. It just breaks my heart."

We each began to weep. And then something beautiful happened. These women held me. They didn't turn from me. And I was able to hold them. Where we each had feared hatred and rejection from others, we found only love, acceptance, and care.

"Jesus died for abortion too," Sandy spoke up.

"He doesn't love you any more or any less," Jill said. "He just loves you."

As we held one another and wept, I felt the love of Jesus Christ enter into the deepest recesses of my heart, the place I had kept closed just for the baby and me.

In that moment, I realized that my child is safe in the arms of the Lord in heaven.

It was over. The anguish, the shame, the mourning, all the dark secrets had finally come to an end. I knew I was forgiven. I am forgiven. I no longer needed to hide from God or anyone else in this life. Throughout this life, our enemy, the devil lives to turn our dreams into nightmares. But this is the exact ground that Jesus Christ comes to redeem.

His forgiveness set me free—not only from my sin, but from believing the lie that I could be like God and control the future. I had chosen abortion to save myself from an uncertain fate as a pregnant woman alone in life. I was learning the truth Jesus taught in Matthew 16:25 that whoever wants to save his own life will lose it. He was talking about eternal life. Faith in God versus self-reliance plays out well before you die. For me, the world of work and radio became a refuge from risking failure at my first love—performing in front of an audience. As a younger woman I had gained admission to Northwestern University's competitive theater department, and I had won competitions as a singer and public speaker. But after abortion, I fell prey to all the insecurities and fear which drive a guilty heart. I stayed in the security of radio, playing out the persona of a false self crafted in my own image and watched my true desire slowly fade away.

I had saved my career, but I was in danger of losing my dream. To sing well you must open your heart first to fully hear the music and then simply sing it back to other open hearts. Anything else rings false. Yet after abortion to risk such openness had seemed impossible, even though my heart still heard God's sweetest songs.

After my experience at the retreat I had a new resolve to do what Jesus said. I began to be more outspoken about my faith in him—I now wanted everyone to know Jesus as I do! This meant that I no longer fit in as well in the world of news radio where I had become established as a talk show host and personality.

But at the same time God began providing opportunities for me to tell of his love, and I began to risk losing the reputation I had crafted over the course of twenty-plus years as a local celebrity. I accepted invitations to tell my story at a Christian recovery center. To my shock, they did not treat me with disgust or keep me at arm's length. When they heard what God's love can do, they stood up and cheered.

As time went on, I stepped back from the daily live radio broadcasts I had been engaged in for over twenty-five years to produce a program which told the truth about abortion. Every week for one year we presented a new story of God's redeeming love in one person's life. And soon after that, I was given the opportunity to create and host a daily talk show on a Christian network of stations.

I hope it builds your faith to see how God's hand took me from one place to the other—redeeming my wrong choice by completely reshaping my world of work.

The Lord may not call you to quit a job or uproot some important aspect of your life. But I can promise you that when his mercy becomes real to you, you will never be the same.

When I left that career to write this book, I was determined to only use my gifts and talents to give voice to God's love. I began to develop my gift through singing lessons. I stopped worrying about where God would take me, and began to let him build my house.

I would wait for invitations to sing, and in the meantime I would sing to Jesus.

The Lord has answered with invitations to sing and lead worship at a Bible study in my church, at a local prison, and at the nursing home where my father-in-law lives. My son, Sam, the marketing mind in our family, suggested a promotional poster to publicize God's gigs for me:

COMING SOON
TO A PRISON OR NURSING HOME
NEAR YOU!

As a former success-driven striver, I now love the idea of a new life of downward mobility for Christ. After all, isn't Jesus coming soon to just the same places in our midst?

That's grace: God giving us the true desires of our hearts, and the good things in life we don't deserve. He is fulfilling my dream to sing, and I have the joy of doing it God's way. And that's mercy: God not giving us the punishment we deserve. He ended my nightmare of the craven fear of judgment by lifting me up to his forgiving love. Singing God's praise has blessed me and contributes to my healing from the spiritual wound of abortion because singing is another way to tell Jesus' story. Music is a powerful antidote to the bitter cocktail of guilt and regret. God often sets singers in the frontline of spiritual progress (see 2 Chron. 20:21)! Songs of praise help heal us by reinforcing our other practices of faith.

"But," you might say, "that seems so far from what I am experiencing. That seems so far from where I am."

I too once said, "But I knew better." I was not a believer in Jesus Christ at the time of my abortion. Even after I believed, it took time for me to come to see God's love, find his mercy, and experience his forgiveness.

Your story may be different. Maybe you were a Christian when you chose to abort. Maybe you knew your choice was wrong, that you were taking a life, and yet you went ahead. Maybe you cannot believe that God can forgive such a choice. You wonder if you will ever be able to trust yourself after such a spectacular failure of faith. You may count your very faith among the losses abortion has cost you, as you ask, "How could God let that happen?"

The more important question is not how he may have allowed that to happen, but do you see how much he loves you and forgives you in spite of anything that's happened or anything that will?

Today I can assure you that nothing is more important than receiving the gift of repentance (2 Tim. 2:25). Seeing God as the one who heals rests upon this point. Up to receiving repentance, you can know and believe, just as he told us in John 14:6, that Jesus is the only way to the Father and heaven. You can accept him as your Savior and start growing in the knowledge of him through Bible reading, worship, and prayer. However, the most important thing is to face Jesus Christ with your own heart, to see his suffering and death for your sake. To hear, as those Roman guards did, his cry of finishing the work to forgive anything you've ever done and anything you'll ever do; to know that's his promise, along with living inside you, making your life new (2 Cor. 5:17).

Love like that requires a response.

Love like that found me at that retreat. It was a holy night when my heart had finally seen the mercy of my Savior, and as the old hymn ("O, Holy Night") foretold, "He appeared and my soul felt its worth."

—— *Reflect* ———————————————————

Read for yourself in Matthew 27, Mark 15, Luke 22–23, and John 19, the accounts of the crucifixion and final hours in the life of Jesus. As you place yourself in the drama, ask who best represents your attitude toward the trial and tortuous treatment of Jesus. Now think upon these passages:

- "For whoever desires to save his life will lose it, but whoever loses his life for My sake will save it. For what profit is it to a man if he gains the whole world, and is himself destroyed or lost?" (Luke 9:24–25 NKJV; see also Matt. 10:39; Mark 8:35; John 12:25).

- "But whatever was to my profit I now consider loss for the sake of Christ. What is more, I consider everything a loss compared to the surpassing greatness of knowing Christ Jesus my Lord, for whose sake I have lost all things. I consider them rubbish, that I may gain Christ and be found in him, not having a righteousness of my own that comes from the law, but that which is through faith in Christ—the righteousness that comes from God and is by faith. I want to know Christ and the power of his resurrection and the fellowship of sharing in his sufferings, becoming like him in his death, and so, somehow, to attain to the resurrection from the dead" (Phil. 3:7–11).

- "Whoever does not love does not know God, because God is love. . . . We love because he first loved us. . . . Everyone who believes that Jesus is the Christ is born of God, and everyone who loves the father loves his child as well" (1 John 4:8, 19; 5:1).

- "Woe to him who builds his realm by unjust gain to set his nest on high, to escape the clutches of ruin! . . . Woe to him who builds a city with bloodshed. . . . Has not the LORD Almighty determined that the people's labor is only fuel for the fire, that the nations exhaust themselves for nothing? For the earth will be filled with the knowledge of the glory of the LORD, as the waters cover the sea" (Hab. 2:9, 12–14).

- "Yet I will rejoice in the LORD, I will be joyful in God my Savior. The Sovereign LORD is my strength; he makes my feet like the feet of a deer, he enables me to go on the heights" (Hab. 3:18–19).

—— *Request* ————————————————————————

O God, your mercy is beyond comprehension. Help me grasp the truth right now that Jesus died to forgive everyone, even me. Help me to know in my bones, to my very core, how far you've gone for me and would have gone for me, even if I were the only one. Help me to love like you do, and to forgive as you do. I pray this in Jesus' name. Amen.

―――― *Respond* ――――――――――――――――――――――――

- Rent a film portraying the death of Jesus Christ such as *The Passion of the Christ*, *The Messiah*, or *Jesus of Nazareth*. As you watch, reflect on the way Jesus suffered and died. What moves you most about his journey from the Last Supper to the cross? Steal yourself away to a quiet place where you can tell him. Think on it as your time with him in the garden of Gethsemane. What are you grateful for in his life and sacrifice?

- If you have accepted Jesus Christ as your Savior, you know that he has forgiven you from all sin. Perhaps though, just as I did, you still need to make him the Lord of your life. Seek the Holy Spirit's guidance as you write about any area of your life which seems more important to you than obeying God as a response to Jesus having given his life in exchange for yours. It might be your career, a relationship, the security of your status in life. Write about what it would mean to you to lose these things for Jesus' sake.

- Keep your heart tuned to sing God's grace with songs about the lengths Jesus has gone to in loving you: the refrain of "The Old Rugged Cross" by George Bennard contrasts how we cherish the cross compared to our earthly measures of success. "Jesus Messiah" by Chris Tomlin lists the glorious attributes of Christ in his power to save. Brian Doerksen's "The River" portrays a washing away of the sins we cannot bear ourselves, and John Newton's classic hymn "Amazing Grace" recounts the joy of being saved from our own wretched way of life apart from Jesus. List your favorite songs of freedom and forgiveness. These songs can carry you whenever you're tempted to condemn yourself, reminding you that ". . . 'tis grace hath brought me safe thus far, and grace will lead me home."

A Restoration

Can you love again?

N o one starts out to take a life when choosing abortion. Many of us simply were trying to make our way in the world. The truth begins to dawn in our minds: abortion may have allowed us to continue on our path, but now we must at last begin to count the human cost.

The resulting turmoil may feel overwhelming. You may not see how you can possibly gain any ground while sorrowing over your loss.

Jesus is a safe place to examine our deepest sorrows, because he is able and willing to comfort the sorrow of every woman who's made her life an utter wreck and ruin. As you leave behind the worldly sorrow of a guilty conscience and take on the godly sorrow of being his beloved and forgiven child, you will find yourself hungry to return to him in love, as one finally finding her way home.

To repent means to change. It means to change your thinking and your heart—to choose to embrace the truth and let go of regret, and choose to let God have his way and allow his Word to transform you from the inside out. This process began for me with the realization that Christ's love in his death on the cross changes everything, even my thinking and my feelings about my child who is no more. The love of Jesus Christ touched my heart to believe and know my child lives on—known by God, loved, and forever safe with him. God's gracious act of mercy inspired in me a love I had never known before, as one forgiven, as one redeemed.

Despite what I had done, Jesus not only held a place for me, but he holds my child in heaven. This grace completely captivated my heart: Jesus has cradled the heart of my child in his arms forever safe in the reality of heaven.

How could I possibly return this debt of love? Could I affirm in God's Word this new reality confirmed in my heart and my mind to be true? And after what I had done, would anyone righteous listen?

Another woman wondered about such things—what embracing the truth could mean for her personally. She wondered how she could possibly be loved after what she had done and how to ask for it, experience it, go forward from it. She longed to give her heart, but wondered, as I have, and maybe you wonder even now, *Can I find faith to follow Jesus wherever his love will lead? Can I let his truth so fully capture my heart as to begin to change my thinking?*

Where His Love Leads

The velvet rope had never been a problem. Once the bouncer's eyes followed her hair falling softly across her bosom, he would always just wave her on through. She couldn't afford the place, but if you wanted to make it, you had to know the scene—and the players. Some girls never made it past the rope, but she had caught on fast. And so she had gone inside.

The men who frequented that place had the means to finance all her dreams. Still, she was shocked when one of them offered her a thousand dollars to go back to his place.

She'd wondered if he was really carrying that kind of cash. Then with guilt realized that she'd seriously considered his offer.

The old man had caressed a stray tress of her hair, a gesture she took for tenderness. He seemed harmless enough.

She'd gone home with guys for nothing before, she reasoned. Besides, she needed the money. Isn't that why she was there?

Looking back now, she wished she had never crossed that velvet rope. Regret doesn't even begin to say it. No one just decides to sell out. It was all so unjust. That man, a man of office, it turned out, was the one who betrayed his constituency and family. Yet all these years later, she still paid the price, wearing the labels CALL GIRL, POLITICIAN'S PROSTITUTE, and worse. She feared she would never live down that past indiscretion. Now she believed no man would risk trusting her love in the future. A ruined reputation also ruins a second chance.

Then she met a truly holy man.

Unlike any other man she'd known, he wanted only to give and bring life to people in despair.

People like me, she thought. When he arrived at a local venue, she took her place in line. She wanted to tell him she had left that life. She also wanted to give him what she had saved up. *Maybe,* she thought, *it is a way I can show I have changed, I am trying to do the right things, I have left behind my old indiscretions, my wrongs.* In any case, she felt sure he would know how to use what she'd been saving for good, and she was ready to give all she had for his belief in her turning from her old life, for his forgiveness. This was the first time she'd ventured into the public eye since her disgrace, and she definitely wasn't trying to call attention to herself. Yet when it was her turn, she fell down at his feet. Through her sobs, she heard the familiar voice of the host of the event, a religious man, a famous television evangelist. Over the noise of the audience reaction, she heard the truly holy man defending her to the famous, religious man.

All she could do was watch her tears collect on the holy man's feet. *Even his feet are too holy for tears from one such as me,* she thought. She tried to wipe them away with her hair. *Please let him forgive me for even this,* she prayed, spreading the money she'd brought at his feet. Then something compelled her to look up. *Was she seeing things? Had her tears affected her vision?*

He looked deep into her eyes with unmistakable love, though he was speaking to that preacher. *She has a loving heart,* he said, *a big heart.* The truly holy man was looking at her intently. "Her many sins have been forgiven," he said, "for she loved much. But he who has been forgiven little, loves little."

He helped her to her feet. "You are forgiven," he said.

A big heart. Forgiven. Loved much. She couldn't understand it, but she'd never known how to love until this man had given unholy her all his holy heart, and in front of all these righteous people. She would never use men again. She would never go back to her old life. She could begin again, even forgive those men who had tried to buy her love.

Some of the people seemed shocked, a few even offended. Everyone knew her reputation.

As she turned to go home, she heard someone mutter, "Who is this so-called holy man to just forgive?"

Where Facing the Truth Leads

In the woman who met Jesus in Luke 7:36–50, others saw a sinner wiping her tears from his feet, but Jesus saw a woman moved beyond reasoning from sorrowing over her wrongs. He understood that she was pouring out a heartfelt emotional response to having been released from the horrible mess she had made of her life, rejoicing over this chance she had found of finally starting over again.

This is what repentance looks like—and for those of us who have chosen abortion, it is the picture of the place we eventually come to—a place of laying our past at the feet of the one who has the power not only to redeem that past, but to transform our present and future too.

We cannot get there until we see our sorrow as God does, coming face to face with the concrete consequences of the abortion we chose: *This affected not just me, and not just some abstract definition of a new life, but a real person, a baby—my baby—a precious and valuable human life.*

That truth can be crushing. The emotional distress of having sentenced our child to die can seem too much to bear.

Such emotional distress over a similarly serious wrongdoing brought the woman who faced Jesus to her knees. She fell there shunned, utterly driven out beyond all hope. And from there Jesus brought her to a place of comfort and relief. Her chastisement was over, he pronounced her pardon complete.

"You are forgiven," he said, illuminating his actions with a parable about forgiving debt (vv. 40–43). Jesus asked Simon, the righteous host of the meeting, who would love more—a person forgiven a great debt or someone forgiven a lesser one?

"I suppose," Simon answered coldly, "the one who had the bigger debt cancelled."

But Jesus didn't want words. He wants our love as the only appropriate response to the love he has lavished on us to die to make us his own. When he approved and forgave the woman fallen at his feet, he was telling everyone that truly grasping the grace of being forgiven forever changes our hearts. And when our hearts are thus changed, we want to pour our love out in return, especially those of us who have fallen a great distance from a righteous way of life. Because, in Jesus, we see that God has come to comfort and speak tenderly to us (Isa. 40:1–2). Even after abortion, our sin has been paid for—a glorious new perspective allowing us to see God's plan for us and for our little ones as well.

Jesus received the sinful woman's embrace as proof that she had stopped fighting the truth. She was no longer lying to herself or anyone else, no longer deceived, and no longer avoiding the judgments of others. Her love for Jesus overrode all that.

Have you yet grasped this great forgiveness and hope which would draw your heart to love Jesus like that?

Reality, Reckoning, and Repentance

The truth that we chose our child's death is hard. It's horrible to even put it this way. But it is true. And facing the reality of our lost children after abortion may be one of the hardest things God will ever ask any of us to face.

Many women weep spontaneously upon seeing an image of a child at twelve weeks gestation, the typical age at which abortion cuts a child's life short. A woman who has undergone an abortion may weep for even more reasons than the wonder of it all.

Molly did. Her cousin's ultrasound pictures made Molly think of what her own baby would have looked like, had she not gone through with an abortion. It was a devastating moment, anticipated for years, that Molly had tried to avoid.

"I hated having any reminders of the abortion," she said. "I dreaded being asked about pregnancies at my annual check-up. Even being around kids was hard for me, but I couldn't avoid my cousin's baby shower. All her friends had chipped in on the cost of a 4D ultrasound before the pregnancy was even showing. When they played the video at the party, I was shocked. What a beautiful face on the screen! All I could think was, *Is that what my baby looked like? What have I done?*

Yet facing those images was the beginning of Molly's healing. They reinforced the truth that she'd hidden in her heart and that was confirmed in God's Word. She had been carrying a baby. She lost a baby. She chose to lose her baby.

Hard as it was facing the truth, Molly says, "That video planted seeds of a complete change of heart about abortion. Guilty sadness always made me wonder if it really was a baby, and I was afraid the Bible proved it. Now I'm so glad I know the truth about my child. I'm beginning to feel like a mother for the first time. God is helping me find love I never knew I was capable of feeling."

But how did she find God's truth to begin with—and how can you?

I made my choice for abortion based on the false perception that it wasn't a child, that it was, as people said, "just tissue." But the perception of a pregnancy as "just tissue," "a parasite," or "potential life" is not accurate according to God's Word or medical science.

Our thoughts drive our spiritual beliefs, and we cannot be fully healed spiritually after abortion until we change our thinking as we repent from following worldly thinking and decide to listen to God's heart for his beloved children.

One shocking example of the divergence of thought between the world and God's Word is our attitude toward children with Down's syndrome. An *ABC News* report said that 92 percent of children with a prenatal diagnosis of Down's are aborted.[1] God would not say that a handicap negates the value of the life of a child. Neither would the joyful parents who have welcomed such children into our world. But the perception of these children as burdensome, coupled with fear, now leads the majority of parents expecting a child with Down's syndrome to abort.

Perceiving unborn children as an expendable hindrance flows from the world's ideas that unborn children are somehow less than fully human. Such wrong thinking about my unborn child allowed me to pursue the ideals of autonomy and independence, rather than God's ideal purpose of choosing life and living a life of love. Abortion also served the purpose of helping me avoid the obligations of parenthood, maintaining my status as a free moral agent, and pursuing my sex life as I saw fit.

But, as Stephen Merritt said, "Moving the hands of a clock to suit you does not change the time."[2] Wrong perceptions cannot change the reality that abortion destroys the actual body and life of another specific person, a full human being formed by God in his very image.

As Randy Alcorn points out, abortion cannot turn back time and make anyone un-pregnant; a child in a mother's womb makes a woman a mother, and makes a man a father.[3]

Facing this truth should trigger both our agony and our repentance. After abortion we are parents—yes, mothers and fathers of children who are now deceased by our own hand.

Your words of regret over past actions and of desire for a right future mean nothing if your heart does not love God enough to sorrow with him over abortion and to allow Jesus to shape your new future in him.

Jesus gave the repentant woman dignity, saying, "Her many sins have been forgiven—for she loved much. But he who has been forgiven little loves little" (Luke 7:47). When you truly love Jesus and pursue his love, you will begin to stop thinking as the world thinks about abortion, and you will be "transformed by the renewing of your mind" (Rom. 12:2). This kind of transformation thoroughly changes your thinking when it comes to abortion, signaling a complete shift from the way the world perceives it and giving us a window into the very heart of God.

Getting to the Truth

The Bible helps us see that our unborn children are known and loved by God because we see that God knows, values, and loves every single individual life; that he has ordained the moment each new life begins; and that he mourns with us the moment of each death.

Perception of life in the Old Testament First we are known by God before he creates us and before he places us in our mother's womb (Jer. 1:5). The Bible tells us God creates a new child, unique in every way from every other human, in three separate and distinct phases (Ps. 139:13–16). Spirit and emotion work together in the innermost being of the unformed body which then takes on a frame, the physical body of the child.[4] God forms us complete with a spirit and emotions as he gathers the raw material of physical life (sperm and egg) to form our bodies. We are spiritual beings who exist beyond the finite terms of life and death, fulfilling God's perfect plan for maintaining oversight of every single moment of every single life.

Perception of life in the New Testament

The Bible is filled with examples of God's perception of life before birth. One is found in the visit of Mary, the mother of Jesus, to her cousin Elizabeth in Luke 1:39–44. Both women were expectant mothers, and the unborn John in Elizabeth's womb leaped for joy. The unborn John had feelings and relationship already with his cousin Jesus, the one he was to prepare a way for in this world. Though the unborn Jesus and John were extraordinary human beings—the Savior and his servant, a prophet—their capacity for human emotion before birth is a capacity we all carry by extension.

God becoming human is a great mystery of our faith that reveals the high value God places on all human life. God willed for his Son, Jesus Christ, to take on human form. C. S. Lewis said, "The eternal being became not only a man but (before that) a baby, and before that a fetus inside a woman's body."[5] When Jesus took on human tissue, he didn't cease from his essential nature as God (John 1:14), nor does our flesh nullify our spiritual being (2 Cor. 5:1).

God's perception revealed today

Why then is there double-mindedness on abortion? To justify abortion, we say that before birth there is just tissue, not a human and spiritual being. And yet our culture accepts and even celebrates the idea of life before birth—with baby showers to gather gifts for a child not yet born.

Expectant parents play music and read aloud to begin teaching children before birth. And we are the first generation in history with ultrasounds to see what God has always seen—the world of the unborn child within a mother's womb.[6] We appear quite eager to take a look. Elective ultrasound facilities with names like *First View* and *Womb with a View* are now so well-established as to offer online streaming of the images, and discount coupons on their websites.[7] Ultrasound mall boutiques allow couples to purchase 3-D or 4-D videos.[8] *NOVA*'s "Miracle of Life" episode remains one of its most popular programs, decades after its original airing on PBS in 1983, and the companion *Windows on the Womb* website has an interactive feature which lets expectant parents track the development of their growing child.[9]

As a society, our actions reveal the truth. We know every pregnancy means we are, as we used to commonly say, "with child."

We've simply moved the ethical line about what we owe to our weak and dependent little ones.

Only the love of Jesus allows us to embrace the truth and agree with God's perspective. His truth put a face on abortion for me—humanizing the face of my child. Somehow my acceptance of the sinfulness of abortion did not prepare me for the magnitude of knowing my abortion was the direct destruction of an actual person, another human being—my own child.

How could I have gone this far? And more, how could Jesus have gone so far to save me?

TIMELESS TRUTH

As we embrace the truth, Jesus' love gives us a completely new perspective on life.

Walking into a Restored Life

It may be painful to admit we were so wrong, to give up all the excuses and defenses put up against the truth. The old mind-set said, "We did the best we could," or, "Abortion was for the best."

Seeking God's best channels our sorrow his way. The worldly sorrow of self-justification is a deadly spiritual and emotional barrier that keeps us from embracing our true justification in Christ alone (Rom. 5:9). Repenting repairs our emotions as God wipes out our sins and refreshes us by sending Jesus, "the Christ, who has been appointed for you" (Acts 3:19–20). This means a repentant change of heart brings the cleansing, refreshing power of God's forgiveness through personal contact with Jesus Christ.

In my case, Jesus didn't want me just to concede that I was wrong, that abortion takes a life. He wanted me to know that he had completely redeemed it all, and that he holds this life, my child, my little one safe in his care.

Be Not Afraid by artist Greg Olsen depicts Jesus standing on a rock in a shallow canyon of rushing waters. He holds an infant high on his left shoulder as his strong right hand powerfully pulls a young girl from the rushing waters beneath her feet. As women who believe in him as Savior, we may have seen Jesus from a distance, as the rocks cut our feet and the rapids pull us under. But as we do the difficult work of repenting after abortion and we find ourselves face to face with his love, we also find something we never dared to dream. Jesus stands smiling, there at the center of a joy-filled meeting with the child we could never know apart from God's mercy and grace.

Not only are we forgiven, but we are given this exceedingly great and precious gift—a child, our child held safe for us within his strong embrace.

Once we hold this truth in our hearts, how can we not fall at his feet and worship him with our love?

Repentance is a highly productive emotional state compared to feeling dead inside when we are weighed down by the past. According to 2 Corinthians 7:8–11, repentance leads our hearts formerly hardened to sin to a new perspective producing earnestness, eagerness to clear ourselves, indignation, alarm, longing, concern, and readiness to see justice done. But staying stuck in our emotional pain keeps us in the shadow of fearing God's punishment and wrath. Worldly sorrow reflects our former dead-end thinking, exhibited with:

- Avoidance
- Guilt
- Shame
- Remorse
- Self-loathing
- Self-justification
- Confusion
- Despair from prolonged mourning

Godly sorrow, on the other hand, flows out of a change of heart that looks like this:

- You face the truth.
- You seek forgiveness.
- You show concern for self and others.
- You have a desire to be cleared.
- You feel indignation over deception.
- You're ready to see justice done.
- You have a deep desire to do right.
- You are now longing with hope for your children.

When our hearts continue to condemn us and abortion leaves us not feeling forgiven, repentance brings peace. Many well-meaning counselors fail to understand why this is so. I've heard many stories:

> "My pastor said I was placing myself above God's forgiveness—he just doesn't get it, and maybe neither do I."

> "I know God forgives me, but I'm still so hurt and confused."

This common emotional reaction to abortion may be rooted in grief and guilt. Unrecognized parental guilt can make forgiveness feel empty and hollow. You think, *If I let go of my pain then it will really all be over and there will be nothing even left to mourn.* Grief unrecognized over unacknowledged loss may cause you to cling to abortion as the only reminder that you were ever a parent of this little one you learned to love too late. *There's a part of me that died,* you tell yourself. *How can I just move on?* Difficult and painful memories of abortion at least affirm that you were, indeed, once a parent, and you may cling to that emotional pain as your only proof.

Godly sorrow leading to repentance produces a blessed resolution to our guilt and grief. God in Christ has promised that all is not lost—not even our children. My heart began to burn to know the biblical truth concerning children who have died because of abortion. I experienced an earnest need to know God's Word. I became eager to search my heart completely so that I could confess everything and be completely cleared of all wrong related to the abortion. I was indignant over how abortion cheapens life, and over all the lies and deception used to sell it to us today. I was alarmed to learn that, according to the *New England Journal of Medicine*, every single day more than 3,500 children will die because of abortion in America.[10] I longed to know Jesus more and to make him known. I grew concerned for young women who are as ignorant as I once was. I wanted to defend all innocent life—those who cannot defend themselves.

This is truly a stunning turnaround in light of the fact that I had no real opinion on the issue until I had an abortion. And even then, until I encountered the love of Jesus on the cross, I continued to think abortion was acceptable, even though I knew in my heart that it must be wrong. But when you encounter the truth and spill out your grief and guilt at Jesus' feet, just as the woman did as she bathed him in her tears, Jesus' love and forgiveness for you then fills you with an overflowing love.

That makes you no different from the woman who spilled her tears at Jesus' feet. Loving God and bowing to embrace his truth is meant to change us. It's meant to show us we had completely lost our way. Like someone lost in the woods, just wishing we had a different compass reading can never help us locate true north. Embracing reality and setting a new course is our only hope. Falling to the feet of Jesus, who can lead us home, is the only way. He is our guide, our spiritual compass, his kindness our door to God's presence and peace.

When we let Jesus lead us then through repentance, new emotions pour forth. Rejoicing replaces grieving and love replaces languishing in guilt, regret, and remorse. We become eager to clear ourselves, alarmed about our sin, determined to stop harming others, and poised to live a new life (2 Cor. 7:10–11).

Holy sorrow is a God-given reflex to teach us God's view of our hearts. As we see that we are forgiven, we gain his power to forgive.

The Lord rewards our desire to trust him by doing the work of changing our hearts and minds so we can live his way (Prov. 3:5–6). As we are forgiven, our changed behavior reflects our embrace of his truth within (Luke 24:45–47).

Jesus provides this pathway to reconciling all the pain of the past. God promises that nothing can separate us from the love of Christ who always lives to pray for us (Rom. 8:34–35). That promise leads you away from the agony of abortion and into a new life.

When you love Jesus much, you are forgiven much.

This is God's loving pathway to encountering his joy.

—— *Reflect* ————————————————————————

Read for yourself in Luke 7:36–50 the story of Jesus anointed by a sinful woman. Isn't it beautiful how Jesus says, "Therefore, I tell you, her many sins have been forgiven—for she loved much. But he who has been forgiven little loves little"? This verse is my life verse—one that helps me set my moral compass to be a loving person in light of God's love for me. Now think upon these Scriptures:

- The Old Testament message of the comforting love of Jesus: "Comfort, comfort my people, says your God. Speak tenderly to Jerusalem, and proclaim to her that her hard service has been completed, that her sin has been paid for, that she has received from the LORD's hand double for all her sins. A voice of one calling: 'In the desert prepare the way for the LORD'" (Isa. 40:1–3).
- Jesus' forerunner, John the Baptist, preached, "Repent, for the kingdom of heaven is near" (Matt. 3:2). Repentance is a promise

of comfort in light of a clear warning against continuing life apart from God.

- Take time to study one or more of the following accounts of people who encountered Jesus and then fell, kneeled, or bowed down at his feet: Peter, James, and John at the Transfiguration (Matt. 17:6), Jairus asking for healing for his daughter (Mark 5:22), the bleeding woman (5:33), lepers (Luke 5:12), Jesus' dear friend Mary at the death of her brother, also Jesus' friend, Lazarus (John 11:32), the witnesses to Christ's arrest in Gethsemane (18:6), and Saul who became Paul (Acts 9:4). Read how even evil spirits fall before Jesus (Mark 3:11; 5:6; Luke 8:28).

- "Or do you show contempt for the riches of his kindness, tolerance and patience, not realizing that God's kindness leads you toward repentance?" (Rom. 2:4).

- "Even if I caused you sorrow by my letter, I do not regret it. . . . Now I am happy, not because you were made sorry, but because your sorrow led you to repentance. For you became sorrowful as God intended and so were not harmed in any way. . . . Godly sorrow brings repentance that leads to salvation and leaves no regret, but worldly sorrow brings death. See what this godly sorrow has produced in you: what earnestness, what eagerness to clear yourselves, what indignation, what alarm, what longing, what concern, what readiness to see justice done" (2 Cor. 7:8–11).

-------- *Request* --

Lord, how I wish you were present physically so I could touch you and show you my great love. I would kiss your feet and stroke your hand. I would ask you where you got such a big heart, how it can hold so much love. It's impossible for me to grasp how much you love me. Help me to love like that. Help me forgive others just as you have forgiven me. I only want to belong to you, and to know that you are mine. In your name, I ask these things. Amen.

─── *Respond* ──────────────────────────────

- Pray for willingness to forgive others. If we hold onto anger in our hearts, Jesus says we are open to the same charge as one who murders (Matt. 5:21–24). Remember, forgiving is a decision you make as a matter of the heart in obedience to God. Caring conversations or careful confrontations may come later, if and when God so leads.

- Confession is a key component to all healing and true release from all sin. The Bible offers this practical advice: "Therefore confess your sins to each other and pray for each other so that you may be healed. The prayer of a righteous man is powerful and effective" (James 5:16). After abortion, it may be hard to identify who this righteous person would be, and harder still to trust. But Jesus reassures us that he will protect us as we come to him in the presence of others. He drew the sinful woman into the presence of righteous people and empowered her to withstand whatever judgment they may have held against her, even in their private thoughts. Begin to develop faith that he will do the same for you as you connect at your church or within your caring circle of Christian friends. There is no substitute for authentic relationships based on God's people coming together to display our love for him publicly. This is part of God's plan for us after abortion. No one is excluded. You may even find that your confession will lead to deeper and closer relationships, not judgment, rejection, or additional pain. Perhaps you will want to prepare your heart for the blessing of confessing to another by first writing your confession to God. When you finish, burn or tear up your letter as an offering to God, who promises to forgive you and cleanse you of sin and remember it no more (Heb. 10:17–18).

- Now take a bolder step: Confess your sins audibly to someone godly and trustworthy. Find a minister, pastor, close trusted friend, or representative of Christ—someone who loves you and loves Jesus. (Resources and immediate help are listed in appendix A.) Tell this person any personal wrongdoing that has led to guilt feelings, how it's affecting you, and what you want from God.

Look at Psalm 38:18 and Luke 15:21 for how simple this decla-
ration of confession can be. Ask the person to whom you share
your confession to pray for your continued healing—your ability
to leave the past behind as Philippians 3:13 says, and continue to
move forward and love like Christ, fully and completely.

- Select a Scripture verse as your life verse. Choose one that sums
  up your faith, or one that touches your heart. Memorize this
  verse—hide it in your heart—and return to God's truth in times
  of trouble or sorrow.

- Praise God for his promise to forgive you. Listen to and sing along
  to "Redeemer, Savior, Friend" by Darrell Evans for help in pic-
  turing Jesus thinking of you personally on his way to the cross.
  "Wonderful, Merciful Savior" by Eric Wyse and Dawn Rogers will
  help you respond to the surprising ability of Jesus, who comforts
  and rescues us from the results of all our wrongs. "Alabaster Box"
  by Janice Sjostran is a vivid portrait of another woman who loved
  Jesus with abandon (see Matt. 26:7).

A Jubilation

Can you believe your baby is in heaven?

You have heard Jesus say your faith in him saves you (Luke 7:50). If receiving the gift of repentance is a requirement for our blessed hope after abortion, what about your unborn child? Even gaining the peace to know you are forgiven of your part in his or her death may leave you to wonder about the child. Where does the eternal spirit dwell? Is heaven an illusion? Will you ever see your baby again? If you do, will the reunion be painful and horrible, or full of love and mercy and healing? How can you know?

For years I wondered these things. I wondered where my baby was, and if I would see my child again. As a believer in Jesus Christ, I have gained faith that through God's mercy I have a home in heaven when I die. Jesus says he prepares a place for all who trust in God (John 14:1–4). Scripture is filled with promises of heaven for those who believe. But where in God's Word can we locate these same promises for our children after abortion? Does God's mercy extend to our children who die before they can form a saving faith in Christ?

By what he demonstrated on earth, Jesus showed that he is not looking for ways to keep people out of heaven. He came to make a way—even for children, even for the worst sinners, and even in the sight of the most scrupulously religious, he came to make a way.

The worst possibility, that I had somehow condemned my baby not only to no life on earth but to a nowhereland in the afterlife, had haunted me for so long. As that darkness finally began to recede, I needed to know that my joy—my hope of heaven for my child—is true.

And then I paid attention to a story I had heard when I was young.

There Are Happy Endings

Seeing the enormous tent stirred the boy's excitement. He remembered sitting under the bright yellow stripes the year before, to see the circus—animals such as he'd never seen on the farms nearby, and people in costumes from all over the world too. Tonight wasn't a circus though, and the patrons' clothes weren't near as fancy as people filed in on the sawdust-lined floor. Still, he had never seen so many Sunday suits in one place. The whole county must be here!

The noise level rose as people quickly filled every seat under the tent. But he could still overhear Momma whisper, "Heaven."

He liked that word. It sounded like *seven*, which was his age, and his favorite number.

Papa whispered too.

They both looked sad. He heard Momma whisper to Papa, "This man is our only hope, short of heaven. We need to be here tonight. They may have killed John, but they cannot kill the truth."

The boy was old enough to understand killing the animals on the farm. Sometimes a calf had to die so you could sell the meat. Once, Papa had to take down a horse with a broken leg. But the boy had never heard of killing a person.

"Who's John?" he whispered.

"Son," Papa said, "he was a good man who never hurt a fly. He gave his whole life to helping people understand God, but when he spoke out against some bad men in town, they had him locked up for nothing, and then they killed him in the jail."

Momma frowned, and Papa stopped talking. The boy wanted to ask a question, but her index finger stood guard across her lips, and he knew better. So he looked around the tent again. Hundreds and hundreds of people pressed in. He spotted a few friends of his with their parents—and he saw babies and kids of all ages, all up past bedtime.

A sudden silence fell as the teacher walked to the front of the tent and sat down. He began to talk just like a teacher in school, but not like any teacher the boy had ever heard. The teacher's voice was kind, but he also looked strong, like one of those kids brave enough to swing out over the river, and just jump right in for a swim. The boy couldn't tell exactly what the lesson was about—he heard the word *divorce*. He knew some kids at school who talked about that. It sounded like something really bad that happens to parents. Seems like just talking about it might have been part of what got that other fellow, John, in trouble.

Around him, people started to mutter and ask questions. Sort of angry questions, like when other kids say, "Let's play," but you can tell by the way they say it that they really just want to boss you.

The teacher wasn't angry at their questions, but his answers stopped the people from talking back. Some people even left.

That's when Momma stood up. "Let's go," she said.

Kids were getting out of their seats all around him. It couldn't be time to leave because the men stayed in their seats. Instead of leaving, mothers went right up to the teacher to ask him to bless their children. Momma was leading him there too, by the hand. Little babies and kids who could just barely walk, and some his age were around them. Some of the children looked weak and sick. Some wore torn, dirty clothes. The teacher smiled the same way at everyone.

Momma was just in front of the teacher now; the closer the boy got, the more he began to feel warm inside. *That's funny,* he thought, but didn't know why. It seemed like something really special was about to happen.

Now it was his turn to come before the teacher, but one man in a suit jumped up and said to the mothers, "All of you sit back down!" Another yelled, "Get back in your seats!" Another said, "Yes, get back. The teacher still has things to say to us, and we all need to pay him heed."

The teacher's face looked like those men made him really mad. He told them to be quiet. "Let the little children come to me," he said. Then he took the boy's hand and pulled him onto his lap along with two or three other kids who started hugging the teacher's shoulders. The boy was so happy that he hadn't missed his turn! It was like sitting on his granddad's lap—he knew he was loved before the teacher ever said a word.

But when the teacher did speak, what he had to say was even better. The words made the boy smile inside, the best words he had ever heard.

"Keep your heart pure and you'll be mine forever," the teacher told the boy. "You will know God's love whenever people hate you and hurt you without any reason."

The boy wondered if the teacher was talking about him, or about what had happened to that man, John.

The teacher read the boy's mind and said to him, "I will not leave you as orphans. I will come to you." Then he hugged the boy and the other children and told all the people: *This is a picture of heaven. Take a look at these children and me together. Every one of you can be part of my circle of love. It's up to you. I welcome you all, but don't make the mistake of thinking that heaven is your idea, or that you decide who gets to live there or not. Heaven is a place where my love will never end. It is a place which is mine to give, and I give it to people with hearts like these.*

It was a night of promises the young boy would never forget.

The Bible Is Not Silent

This story is not fiction. It is real. The account in Matthew 14–19 shows how that teacher, Jesus, showed extraordinary compassion for children and little ones throughout his traveling ministry. He loved the farm boys and girls in the countryside, and he loved the children in the cities. Everywhere he went, he showed us how to love children like he did, without condition, with open arms, and in the midst of any trouble.

In fact, Jesus was a great defender of children, and the accounts in Matthew 14–19 came at a time of unrest. His cousin, John the Baptist, had been murdered in a grisly and unwarranted way. Jesus himself was under attack by religious leaders of the day, the Pharisees, who thought him a heretic. They peppered him with questions about marriage and divorce, in hopes that he would answer in ways that showed him defying not only their own religious laws but also the Romans' civil laws (Matt. 19:1–12). The Pharisees wanted to be rid of Jesus because his teachings on spiritual freedom and a new way of living by loving were not religion as usual. His teachings were revolutionary, centered in grace, not law.

And it was in this context that Jesus showed his love to children to demonstrate his kingdom's priorities—love over law.

Laurie had wandered far from the practice of her faith when she went away to college, but she had always held onto what she had been taught when she was a little girl—that everyone needs to be baptized in order to get to heaven.

"At my religious school, I was shown how to baptize a newborn baby just in case a little brother or sister became mortally ill or injured in an accident," she recalled. "Of course, as a second-grader, I had no grasp of life and death or the true meaning of baptism. But I got the message: Baptism was an essential practice for all people of faith and the baby's eternal life depended on it."

Laurie chose abortion three times as a young woman adrift in a series of poor relationships. At thirty, she returned to the church, married, and settled down. She knew she was forgiven and she knew she would never choose abortion again, yet whenever there was a baby being baptized, she was troubled.

Her church teaches that baptism removes our human sinful nature due to original sin, and her babies never had that chance. *What hope do I have that I will ever see my children in heaven?* Laurie wondered.

As I studied God's Word and the doctrines of the church, I wondered, *If everyone needs to confess faith in Jesus Christ as their resurrected Lord and Savior in order to receive eternal life, how can God accept anyone too young to form such faith?* It is a question that goes straight to the heart of the character and ministry of Jesus Christ. To know the answer, you must know him.

Maybe you understand Laurie's anguish because of your understanding of the doctrine of original sin, or your church's teaching on infant death and baptism. In my case, relying on a remnant of incomplete teaching I recalled only led to deep confusion about the promise of heaven for my child. As my emotions grew more tender, I felt that innocent children deserve to go to heaven and don't deserve to go to hell—but as I searched out answers, I learned the Bible is largely silent on the question of infant salvation or salvation for children who die before birth.

Many sensitive Christians decide that since the Bible is silent, they will be as well.

"Why are Christians so afraid to speak about heaven with those who need to know?" a young mother remarked after the funeral for her toddler who died from complications of pneumonia. "People seemed to be afraid of making it worse," she said, "but the worst thing is withholding words of comfort to parents who miscarry or suffer the deep pain of stillbirth or early infant death."

One pastor recalls his first emergency call to help the family of an infant who had just died. Without a great deal of experience, knowledge, or reflection, the pastor looked across the crib to the devastated young mother and said, "Your baby is in heaven. He is safe in the arms of God."[1]

Later, he worried that perhaps he had misspoken. The parents he spoke to clearly received comfort from his words, but he, himself, did not have a solid foundation of knowledge to support this truth from God's Word.

He began to drill into the Scriptures. Did the Bible really assure this? Was it true? And then he attended a Bible conference where a panel of experts discussed what happens to babies when they die. His three fellow pastors essentially answered, "I don't know."

He determined to do better.[2] Surely God wants us to know.

We glean truths as we examine Jesus' interaction with children in the Scriptures. When his own disciples wanted to keep away the children, Jesus became indignant (Mark 10:13–16). The word *indignant*, meaning "showing anger because of something unjust,"[3] is seldom applied to Jesus. When he was being disrespected, degraded, and killed, Jesus withheld indignation. He didn't even enter into a defense at the unjust trial he suffered before he was put to death (see Mark 15:5). Yet devaluing children caused Jesus to be upset and righteously angry.

Jesus may have been making a statement on the prevailing culture of his day which devalued children through the common and widespread practices of child abuse and child abandonment.[4] How comforting to think that in the midst of our devaluation of the lives of children by our culture's practice of abortion, Jesus is here, saying, "Let the children come unto me." He loves them and is ready to defend, protect, and make a place for them by his side, in his arms.

Look at account after account of this in the Bible, which is filled with moments of Jesus giving little children unmerited favor. He healed them (Matt. 17:14–18), even children not of his tribe (Matt. 15:21–28). He blessed them (Mark 10:16). He gave them a role in his ministry (John 6:9–11). He raised them from the dead (Luke 8:41–56). He caused joy in an unborn child to let us know even before birth children are capable emotional witnesses of truth (Luke 1:44). The entire life and ministry of Christ is an example of mercy and tender care to children.

Knowing that children are always in Jesus' heart, you see it is his will that they should gain heaven by God's good grace. He says it himself even: "'Let the little children come to me, and do not hinder them, for the kingdom of God belongs to such as these. I tell you the truth, anyone who will not receive the kingdom of God like a little child will never enter it.' And he took the children in his arms, put his hands on them and blessed them" (Mark 10:14–16). God even uses a little child as an example for adults in Matthew 18:2–3. Since adults are instructed to become "like little children" in order to enter God's kingdom, we are confident in believing that these little children are accepted into God's kingdom.

I'm grateful for a wise friend who led me to the story of King David who suffered the death of an infant son. In his grief David said, "I will go to him, but he will not return to me" (2 Sam. 12:23). Since David was a man after God's own heart, he must have believed in his own hope of eternal life. Going to the deceased child would mean arriving at the same place of eternal rest. David seems to have known that God has ordained a place of honor for the weakest members of the human family. He consoled himself as a grieving parent with the hope of a blessed and heavenly reunion with his helpless beloved child.

Later in his ministry, after he had gained some prominence in the

Christian community, the pastor I mentioned above was called to appear on national television. He was asked to speak about the truth of heaven after a tragedy that tested the nation's faith. With confidence, having examined many of the biblical accounts like Jesus and the children, this pastor was able to affirm the true and full hope of heaven. Children are there, he could say with confidence, grace, and love.

This pastor is the Rev. John MacArthur, and he tells of learning about heaven, and children's place in it, in his book *Safe in the Arms of God: Truth from Heaven About the Death of a Child*. His evidence begins by discerning God's character, "Throughout Scripture, the Lord's heart seems especially tender toward children."[5]

Though humankind is sinful, MacArthur says, "infants are not culpable in the same sense as those whose sins are willful and premeditated. Therefore, even in the Old Testament, God expresses serious displeasure toward the people of Israel, who failed to treat their little ones the way God treated them."[6]

He points out that God calls children *mine* (Ezek. 16:20–22), and he regards them as innocent and pure.

As MacArthur puts it, "God does not use the word *innocent* unless he means it. . . . God is just and will not punish the innocent."[7] He concludes: "The Scripture weighs very heavily toward the fact that innocent children are in heaven, redeemed and dwelling in the presence of God. . . . God's Word says representatives of [all] tribes and tongues will be in heaven. How is this possible? One way is through the redemption of their little ones. These will be among those who are made 'kings and priests to our God' (Rev. 5:10)."[8]

Isn't that a beautiful reality? Doesn't that ease some of your worst fears of where your baby is now and will be forever? Jesus says, "Come unto me," to your child lost in abortion too. Doesn't it make you long to join your baby there, reunited in love and mercy, without malice or hurt or anger, and in the presence of God?

TIMELESS TRUTH
Jesus, the Christ, the king of heaven, welcomes all little children as his own.

God's gift of heaven for an aborted child may seem like a mystery, but it is also true. He has given us the Bible that we may know him and the mystery of saving grace. It is a spiritual truth requiring no further proof. To believe only that which can be proven requires no faith at all. God's mysteries do not cancel out our faith, they affirm the truth. We're assured, "No, we speak of God's wisdom, a wisdom that has been hidden and that God destined for our glory before time began" (1 Cor. 2:7).

In both humility and hope, our heart's cry as parents of children who have died celebrates that mystery and moves beyond the burden of doubt.

Heaven Is Real

When I confessed my abortion to my friends at the retreat and found God's forgiveness, I immediately gained this knowledge that my child was with Jesus in heaven. Something else happened within my heart that day as well. I felt the spirit of my granny, who went to heaven many years ago, say to my heart, *Welcome home.* It was as though the person who had loved me best knew my heart was finally in the right place regarding God and my unborn child.

Imagining the joy of heaven and the unconditional love of God can be hard to accept if you grew up with parents who were punishing or emotionally impaired or disengaged. You may have suffered neglect or abuse—the opposite of a warm and welcoming embrace. For you to grasp God as our loving Father, you too may need to think of a grandparent or some other warm, kind, and accepting person from your childhood. And for me, the best and most reliable source of love was my Granny.

One day during our chores, she suddenly exclaimed, "My Kimmy! You're a piece of bread!"

I was six years old, and I had no idea what she meant, but I knew I was loved. That's why it was so meaningful to sense her presence in a holy and heavenly circle of love with my child in heaven.

You see, our family moved and Granny and I weren't as close as I became a young woman. She came for a visit the summer I turned nineteen, and I didn't give her much of my time—I was busy with my life. But she was there when my boyfriend sent nineteen dozen sweetheart roses for my birthday.

As the delivery boy kept returning with vase after vase, Granny looked at me and said, "Ain't they beautiful! Now, you enjoy them, and tomorrow send them up to the church."

Her lifelong piety was no surprise and certainly no joke, yet I laughed and said, "The church?! I don't think so."

She paused just long enough to truly catch my gaze before she said, "I'm so sorry you fell away from the things of God. I'm going to pray that he will lead you back to the church."

Her rebuke silenced me, but my foolish and immature heart answered back, "Whatever."

We never regained the closeness that I had counted on as a little girl. As Granny's health declined, distance made the loss of her company and her eventual death seem natural. I hadn't ever really thought of her as living on in heaven. But I believe her prayer for me to return to God, though long forgotten by me, was answered by God on that day at my retreat when Jesus placed such love directly into my heart for my child lost to abortion. I had come back home to an eternal joy and hope that I had never even dared to dream of until God's love made the hope of heaven real in my life. Even though I had long since accepted Jesus as my Savior, on that day something very special happened—I entered God's larger family with *my* family in heaven when I bowed to Jesus Christ as the Lord of my life.

Such wonders only happen within our innermost spiritual hearts, just as it is only by the Holy Spirit that anyone can call Jesus "Lord" (1 Cor. 12:3). And once we do, Romans 8:16 says, "The Spirit himself testifies with our spirit that we are God's children," meaning we share everything Jesus has in his glory in heaven—a realm lovelier by far than the loveliest places on earth, without death or even the threat of death, where we will live fully free, healed, redeemed, and whole.

This hope is yours to claim today. What I sensed about my child in heaven is true according to Scripture, and true for every child lost to abortion. Our children are safe forever with Jesus in heaven, the holy place where God was and is and always will be.

With his dying human breath, Jesus says on the cross to the thief crucified along with him, "Truly, I tell you, today you will be with me in paradise" (Luke 23:39–43). With these words, Jesus proved heaven is not granted to us on the basis of our good works, including baptism; nor is heaven withheld from wrongdoers who repent. The thief on the cross received both mercy and grace, our twofold hope after abortion. Jesus' mercy withheld the punishment the man deserved, and his grace rewarded him a gift he did not earn.

Did you catch that? *God grants mercy.*

It may not meet our expectations for God to give a last-minute reprieve to someone who causes a great deal of suffering in this life. But Jesus said this thief, who was a common criminal guilty of a lifetime of wrongdoing, entered heaven by Jesus' sovereign decree. Mercy is Christ's to give as the reigning king of heaven. The decision about who enters heaven always rests in the hands of Jesus Christ alone (John 9:35–10:30; 2 Cor. 5:10). It is a judgment call, and Jesus is the ultimate judge. The only way to God in heaven is through him (John 14:6). Instead of yielding to guilty fears, or basing our hope on sentimental wishes, when it comes to heaven, we must listen to what Jesus says.

God gives grace.

You may feel overwhelmed by your accountability in the loss of your child's life, but this is also God's ground for great joy.

Whenever I am tempted to think of the what-ifs, or someone contests that babies are not in heaven, I think of the Israelite children, too young to "know good from bad," and how they too were given the Promised Land, even as God prohibited their parents because of sin (Deut. 1:39).

God has the right to give his mercy over and above our understanding (Exod. 33:19), just to renew us as his children (Job 33:23–25). Children have no willful rebellion against God, nor willful unbelief, nor willful sinful action; thus God has no charge against them (see John 3:36).

The salvation of every person is a matter of God's grace, not man's works. Even as we make a profession of faith and experience baptism, these beautiful acts of faith are founded on God's unmerited favor to us

(Eph. 2:8–9). No one can even profess that Jesus is Lord except by the power of the Holy Spirit (1 Cor. 12:3). We are saved by the sacrificial work of Jesus Christ on the cross, justified only by his grace (Rom. 5:9–11; Titus 3:7). Baptism with the Holy Spirit is accomplished only by Jesus (Mark 1:8), not by man.

This is mercy and this is grace. And this is cause for jubilation! There is nothing that your child needed to accomplish or receive in order to enjoy the company of heaven. This is the sure mystery of God's grace.

"[God] will wipe every tear from their eyes," the Bible promises us. "'There will be no more death or mourning or crying or pain, for the old order of things has passed away.' He who was seated on the throne said, 'I am making everything new!'" (Rev. 21:4–7).

Everything is new. Our great and gracious Savior, who changed water into wine to reveal his glory, is able to make our children new in their essential nature as he makes them holy in heaven.

Our children are holy. They are in heaven. And they are held in the loving embrace of Jesus Christ.

And he knows each one by name.

—— *Reflect* ──────────────────────────────────

How Jesus loves the little children! Read for yourself in Matthew 18 his defense of their position in his kingdom and each child's value as a person. To get the full picture of what such teaching could have cost Jesus, read Matthew 14–19. Now think upon these Scripture passages:

- The prophet Isaiah foretold heaven after God judges the earth with justice for the oppressed, bringing peace in the aftermath; heaven is the peaceable kingdom where the lion and lamb lie together, "and a little child will lead them" (Isa. 11:1–6).
- The holy one of heaven, Jesus Christ, came to earth as a child, and first as an unborn child within the womb of Mary. God in human form was first a little child (Luke 1).
- Jesus said heaven is a place where childlike faith will rule: "[Jesus] called a little child and had him stand among them. And he said:

'I tell you the truth, unless you change and become like little children, you will never enter the kingdom of heaven'" (Matt. 18:2–3).

- Jesus promised us a heavenly home: "Do not let your hearts be troubled. Trust in God; trust also in me. In my Father's house are many rooms; if it were not so, I would have told you. I am going there to prepare a place for you. And if I go and prepare a place for you, I will come back and take you to be with me that you also may be where I am. You know the way to the place where I am going" (John 14:1–4).

—— *Request* ———————————————

Lord, I believe you have all authority to grant your kingdom to those you love and accept as your very own, including those who have been utterly rejected and denied their dignity in this life. Lord, help my unbelief concerning the mysteries of heaven. Open up your Word to me as I read your promises and open up my heart to you as I seek your face. I also believe you have forgiven me, by your unmerited mercy, of all the sin attached to abortion, and any other sin that I have yet to confess. Help me to see that I need not fear a painful meeting with my child(ren) lost to abortion. Help me see my heart as you do, so that I may submit to your will and so somehow attain to the resurrection of your glorious body in heaven. Please help me to understand and grasp the mystery of your mercy and grace, in Jesus' name. Amen.

—— *Respond* ———————————————

- Build your knowledge by reading outside sources for biblical perspectives on heaven. Several books are listed in appendix A.
- Though it may be painful to consider, it is stated in God's Word that some adults will *not* go to heaven because of willful rejection of God's love (see Rom. 1). Take time to search your heart now and decide whether you agree that God deserves to exercise judgment of those who reject him in their hearts. Consider whether God is calling you to accept the rite of baptism as a way to affirm your

faith in Jesus Christ. Call on your pastor, priest, or friend in faith today to discuss this important step of faith.

- Now read what the Bible says about heaven in these Scriptures: 1 Corinthians 2:9 (no mind can comprehend it), Isaiah 35:5–6 (a place of wholeness, bliss, and peace), and Revelation 21:3–4 (God's presence forever, without crying, pain, or death). Do these images match your impression of heaven? Why or why not? Have images from art, films, books, or drama shaped your picture of heaven?

- How has your perspective of heaven changed over the years? How did you imagine it as a child? When you first became a Christian? Now? What does it look like? Who is there? Write down what you love most in the Bible descriptions and why, along with your greatest wish for heaven—what you look forward to most. Keep this prayer in a place where you can remind yourself of all God is preparing for you.

- Take time to meditate on the idea from Ecclesiastes 3 that God has set eternity in our hearts—we all yearn for heaven. How would your life today be different if you began to think of heaven as the ultimate reality and this world as but a moment in time? Who will you hope to meet there? Share your faith right here and now as a way to make the invitation to someone you love to be welcomed into the family of God.

- Listen to these songs or sing along as you contemplate heaven and how Christ will be your greatest joy there: "I Can Only Imagine" by Bart Millard, "Tears in Heaven" by Eric Clapton, "With Hope" by Steven Curtis Chapman, and Celine Dion's "A Mother's Prayer." "In Christ Alone" by Keith Getty and Stuart Townsend inspires faith in every season of life. Read through the lyrics in a hymnal for the pictures of heaven in these hymns: "Blessed Assurance," "Be Thou My Vision," "Abide with Me," and "Amazing Grace."

Part Three

The Whole Heart

A Consolation

Where have you laid him?

G rief is a language our hearts will have to learn if we ever want to find true peace after abortion. As the parent of a child whom you cannot see and hold, you have reason for sorrow and sadness; yet accepting you are a parent also opens you up to experiencing and expressing a parent's love and affection for your deceased child. But how do you grieve, how can you mourn when that death, your loss, is something you've tried to hide, and the person you have lost is also one you have never met? Our culture offers few rituals or traditions to help support those who have lost children in miscarriage or stillbirth, let alone abortion. Can your mourning of an abortion, without surrounding sympathy, ever end?

Jesus joins your sadness and understands such questions. He knows how to help you revisit the experience of losing and mourning someone loved and lost in a formal and dignified way. He also knows how to love us in a way that conquers death, building a bridge between us and the hearts of our children. And he shows us how.

Calling Out Buried Grief

"I'm afraid you'll have to wait here."

The nurse was gentle, but her words landed like a blow when the crisis team arrived to take her brother for emergency help. Hours later, this room echoed an eerily quiet calm as again Mary surveyed the sink and medical instruments. She had time to memorize the surroundings. And wait.

The more time passed, the further these things seemed to fall short of what was needed to save her brother's life. But help was on the way. She thanked God once again that her close friend was the best heart doctor in the nation, a remarkable healer and longtime family friend even before he gained a reputation as the physician of last resort.

"I love the man," Mary whispered to herself, thinking of the physician. "I just never thought I would need him like this."

Hope, desperation, and exhaustion mingled in equal measures as she sent word for her great friend to come in her family's hour of need. Her brother was fading quickly. But she knew he could help her brother as no one else could—he had a track record of turning around what other doctors considered lost causes. He had brought back to full health a young girl dangerously close to death. Legends were already being told of how her friend's advice and wisdom were enough to help people heal in remote locations. No case was too difficult, it seemed. But he was also one of the most sought-after doctors in the world. Would he be able to arrive in time?

As day turned into night, her sister arrived from accompanying their brother to Intensive Care. "Let's go home," she'd urged at last. "We both need to get some rest."

Mary was weary. She took her sister's advice reluctantly, leaving her beloved brother, but wondering if she was doing the right thing. "Please, God," she prayed once more, "let him live."

But he did not.

Three days after the funeral, Mary woke from a grief-soaked stupor to hear that the healer had at last arrived.

"He is promising our brother will live," her sister said.

Live? Mary almost laughed with incredulity. *He's already dead! What good could the great physician's visit do now?* She knew he could have helped. Her faith in him had never wavered. But death is death . . . and yet the physician loved her brother too. She pulled herself together to greet their friend.

He had traveled days to get here, and she was grateful to see him, but all she could think to say was, "If only you had been here, my brother would not have died."

His face displayed such sadness! His tears spoke pure grief, not only over the death and his own broken heart, but everyone else's in the room too. "Where have you laid him?" he asked.

She had vowed never to return to the crypt after it had been sealed. But with tear-stained cheeks, she agreed to show her friend. The whole family went, and friends, neighbors—all who were grieving, along with some who were purely curious and others deeply skeptical.

"After all," one man muttered, "that great physician can't be so great—he didn't save this one, did he?"

Once at the burial ground, the physician told the stunned crowd to open the crypt.

Mary watched as some men went to do as her friend had asked. She and her sister believed God would raise the dead again one day. *But today? Would he? Could he?* She wondered, heart racing, as she heard her friend pray, his own face tear-stained, that their lack of faith would not limit the glory of God.

And then she heard him call her brother's name. She saw her brother walk out of the tomb into the sparkling sunshine of this new day.

Going Where Your Grief Is Buried

In this story (from John 11:1–44) Mary and Martha saw their dead and buried brother, Lazarus, raised to new life by Jesus. Only Jesus, the great physician and friend who said, "I am the resurrection and the life" (John 11:25) could make that happen.

Jesus knew that, like Mary, we need to see his almighty power in action. That's why he asked where Lazarus had been buried, and invited everyone present to see his power over life and death—in order that he might give them a glimpse of the glory of God (John 11:40).

In raising Lazarus, Jesus shows us how to not only find our new hope of life, but to go with him to revisit the place of our grief. Just as Mary saw that faith is what matters most when you may feel it least, we can see that Jesus is there, cradling our hearts even into the shadow of death (Ps. 23:4).

This place of grief, the hidden part you've buried, is where your faith alone must carry you. This is where you find God's love and see he has sent Jesus, the great physician, to bring you the new life you so desperately seek—after standing with you to bury the old. But you have to see that Jesus is doing that. You have to acknowledge he wants your faith in him to do that. Faith, after all, is not only for salvation in the life to come—our faith brings riches in the midst of our current trials and troubles as well. Oswald Chambers suggests that taking a step of faith to see Jesus at work in our lives is something not every believer may experience:

> Being saved and seeing Jesus are not the same thing. Many are partakers of God's grace who have never seen Jesus. . . . Jesus must appear to your friend as well as to you, no one can see Jesus with your eyes. Severance takes place where one and not the other has seen Jesus. You cannot bring your friend unless God brings him. Have you seen Jesus? Then you will want others to see Him too.[1]

After his resurrection, Jesus appeared to his eleven disciples many times, but often they did not know him or see him for who he is. They were so heartbroken and overcome with grief. You read in Matthew's gospel how even his closest followers greeted his appearance with worship and yet, "some doubted" (28:17). The risen Lord had to rebuke the eleven for a "lack of faith and their stubborn refusal to believe those who had seen him after he had risen" (Mark 16:14). And in Luke 24, you read how Jesus met his grieving friends on the road to Emmaus, walking and talking with them in their grief. But "they were kept from recognizing him" (Luke 24:16). Only later, while eating supper with him, were their eyes opened and they recognized him.

It takes faith to see the Lord and then to follow him as he accompanies us to a place of grief.

Joanna experienced this need to utterly rely on Jesus in faith. She turned to abortion multiple times in her youth. She hid her grief, and thought she had buried it by keeping it secret. Then she met a good man and they decided to marry. They were eager to begin a family together, but time passed and no children came. When they went to consult their doctor over the fertility issues, all the grief she thought she'd buried came to life again.

She remembers thinking, *How am I going to walk out of this room and tell my husband that he has been so good to me, but now, because of all those abortions that he had nothing to do with, he's not going to have his own biological children?*

"I think it took me an hour to get dressed," she says. "Suddenly my abortions affected him. How was he going to forgive me?"

Bill could forgive because he loved Joanna. He knew her past and loved her anyway. He loved like Jesus, who knows our past and loves us anyway. He showed Joanna there could be new life in Christ and they began to build a family through adoption. But first, he helped Joanna grieve and memorialize the pain of the babies who died in abortion.

"Bill's love for me is just like Jesus' love," Joanna says now. "God throws our sins as far as the east is from the west, never to remember them again. And Jesus is holding my children in heaven, where one day I will get to see them and know how he has cared for them."

Memorializing the Pain Instead of the Child

It would be much easier if everyone around us helped those of us grieving abortion. Unfortunately, quite the opposite happens. Too much of public opinion dehumanizes our children who died by abortion, and that not only robs us of their lives, but also rules out healthy feelings of guilt or grief. You can't grieve a death if you don't agree there was a life. "Reproductive choice" shouldn't hurt anyone. But abortion viewed as "family planning" leaves the parent's heart to grieve secretly. And even in church circles, discussions with those who fail to see the loss of an aborted baby will also likely prove unhelpful in easing the emotional pain.

Perhaps your experience in the church has left you feeling as though you must grieve secretly. Many women don't want anyone at church to know, and this may be in part because not enough people there show Jesus' unconditional love like Bill. And the fear of rejection keeps many parents silent. Many of us are simply overwhelmed and in too much pain to ask for help. You can't grieve a death if no one is willing to talk about it.

What happens is you're left feeling misunderstood or in doubt of Christ's power to call forth life and grieve its loss. As you turn your grief inward you begin to think: *I can't seem to get over this. There must be something wrong with me, in my mind, in my choice, in my heart.*

Counselor Teri Reisser, the author of *A Solitary Sorrow*, says this shame over grief is separate from the shame of sin, and it leads many women to feel defective after abortion:

> Even though abortion is probably the most common medical procedure done in America today, it is something that is experienced in a very solitary fashion because there is so much shame attached to an abortion procedure and decision that women simply don't talk to each other. So they go through this sadly common experience thinking that they are very defective. They're never feeling free to talk about it with other people and so they really do experience it as a solitary experience.[2]

Believing there is no child to mourn, instead you memorialize the pain of your loss.[3] That pain may come to represent your child, since the sorrow may be the only reminder you have that your child ever existed. Essentially, that is getting your emotional wires crossed.[4] You mistake grief for guilt, and you punish yourself to atone. You hang onto that unexamined pain as a way to commemorate the experience of having been a parent. At the same time, as any normal parent wanting love from their child, you have this ache. The ache, somewhere deep in your heart, is for your unborn child. Only there is no outlet, no child present, and none acknowledged as lost. Your grief becomes the sum of the relationship between your aborted child and you. This is an ache that seems only to deepen. Essentially, this ache is unrequited parental love.

Greeting Abortion As Loss

There is a better way to grieve and mourn and live again. But you can only get through the pain, to that new life, by following Jesus Christ and keeping your eyes on him. Christ's invincible love provides the bridge of heavenly hope.

And believing in God's mercy helps you mourn.

Reisser has identified the unique challenge of resolving a grief which is so heavily mingled with our parental guilt. In *A Solitary Sorrow*, she writes:

> Awareness of the need to grieve the loss of an *aborted* child is almost nonexistent in our culture. It is thus very common for post-abortion women to approach the grieving process with trepidation and confusion. "How do I grieve the death of a child when I was the executioner?" they ask. They do not feel they have any right to a normal grieving process. But they also harbor mixed emotions because they *do* grieve for the lost child.[5]

And, she notes, parents may experience a special anxiety for having denied a child the chance for life:

> When you have an abortion you have this terrible, terrible unresolved issue between you and your child. How do you imagine yourself now, dying, going to heaven and facing your aborted child?[6]

Finding God's love allows you to honor the memory of your child and grieve with hope, even as the Lord redeems the difficult details of the day and the way your child has died. Jesus Christ is aware of all that has happened. He is a faithful witness who is able by his love to redeem all sin in order to fit us for his kingdom in heaven (Rev. 1:5–6). This redemption finds fruition as we embrace our child's memory in order to bid them goodbye.

Without Jesus it might even be unwise and unproductive to look back. But he has a good purpose when he asks where we have laid our memories, for "we know that in all things God works for the good of those who love him, who have been called according to his purpose" (Rom. 8:28). By revisiting the place we have left our children, as we go with Jesus, we may finally be able to release our child to rest in peace.

——————————— TIMELESS TRUTH
The love of Jesus Christ, stronger than death, provides a bridge of heavenly hope.

Giving Honor and Dignity

When, like Mary, I determined to follow Jesus to where I thought I had buried my grief and memories, I knew this meant also choosing the company of all those who would mourn with me. As I'd seen in the story of Lazarus, I knew there would be others then who could support and care for me. Their loving presence made it safe to finally risk retrieving the memory of the day of my baby's death. I had worked so hard to forget, would I now be overwhelmed? The pain of not knowing seemed worse.

As I prayed for God to heal the emotional sting of recalling such painful memories, I discovered a document that serves as my memoriam: A handwritten receipt, dated June 16, 1978, noting the address of the abortion facility and a fee of $165.00 paid in full, in cash. This death record, tucked away in a journal, stood unread for many long years as the only evidence my child in fact had ever existed.

Today, I thank God for that silent witness of my child's life and death, for that single slip of paper, that one remnant answered Jesus' question, "Where have you laid him?" (John 11:34).

Knowing the answer helped me revisit the circumstances of that death, but this time going with Jesus and sympathetic friends in faith, who helped me learn to grieve my baby's precious, lost life.

To some people, retrieving such painful memories, the memories of a child lost to abortion, may seem a strange ritual. But it's not. It is right and proper for all parents of deceased children to revisit their grief. And

Jesus goes with us to revive our child in memory, healing that memory by binding up the wounds of our hearts (see Isa. 61:1–3). And he urges us to take others with us to help us and guide our grief along the way.

What company will go with you to mourn your child?

Find your crowd of fellow partakers

About two years after I was redeemed of the abortion, I found these friends in faith when I attended a Bible study support group where I also found peace with the child I know God holds in heaven.[7] I wish that I had taken this step sooner because this group was the pathway to joy that I had never even dared to hope possible. I want you to know this joy and to be able to celebrate your child's life. This group encouraged me as together we discovered that silent grief only multiplies; listening and leaning on each other lightens each other's burden, bringing hope.

I received not only the blessing of being affirmed, but also the gift of time and space to think, remember, and pray with others who would grieve with me. The structure of this group helped me regain trust while creating healthy new relationships as in turn we each created healthy relationships with our deceased children through the love of Christ and the power of the Holy Spirit. The process began as we prayed to know the sex of our child, so we could name that child. This act in and of itself was healing; having a name confers honor and dignity. We would also use our babies' names as we prepared to pay tribute to their lives at a memorial service.

That's right: a memorial service. We were encouraged to enter into rituals and rites to grieve the children we never got to hold in our arms. Toward that end, there were steps I needed to go through in recognizing my baby. Though I had rejoiced over locating the date and other details of the day my child died, I still did not have a sense of whether the child I aborted was a boy or a girl (although with later pregnancies I had a very strong and correct sense of the sex of both of my living children).

After deep reflection, I realized a certain vagueness regarding the sex of my child protected me from the hurt of knowing that I did, indeed, carry a little boy or little girl—a true being, a real life. This was hard to admit too, because it meant I was responsible for taking that life.

Reluctantly, then, I followed the group instruction and began asking God if he wanted me to know whether I have a son or daughter in heaven, and if he would please give me that knowledge. I prayed many days without sensing an answer or gaining insight.

Name your baby

The week before the memorial service, our group attended a silent retreat, spending time with the Lord to prepare our hearts. Some of us wrote poems or made journal entries of our emotions and thoughts. Some walked in the nearby woods. I chose a place of solitude for a frank and honest discussion with God about my sexual history. Practicing complete openness before the Lord, I put aside shame as I turned my gaze toward a wintry sky. I spoke frankly to Jesus. Beginning at my earliest sexual memory, I admitted any thoughts, words, and actions with sexual implications no matter how distant or small. I shared with him things I hope no other human will ever need to know. I wept. I poured out my soul. This was agonizing—to admit the things done in darkness. But it was such a release too. When the flood subsided, God gently quieted my heart as his mercy covered every deficit in my character, and carried it all away.

I have never felt so clean.

When I emerged from the solitude, I opened my Bible to resume my daily reading from the previous day. I read, "Therefore the Lord himself will give you a sign: The virgin will be with child and will give birth to a son, and will call him Immanuel."

Immanuel.

This passage in Isaiah 7:14 foretold the birth of Jesus Christ, and cannot simply be borrowed to mean anything else. Yet God used these words about his one and only Son to minister to me in a profoundly personal way. He gave me a name, *Immanuel*, which means *God with us*. I pondered this name and took it from God as a gift to me so I may know that I, too, have a son in heaven. The name is so fitting; knowing my baby died at twelve weeks gestation in June, I marveled at how my son would have been born close to Christmas. The rejoicing that comes each year during the Christmas season has taken on a special meaning for me. God always finds a personal and surprising way to turn our sorrow into something beautiful wherever our hearts may find his love.

Keep your eyes on Jesus

As the name for my child means, I learned God is indeed with us. Christ comes to us and asks, "Where have you laid him?" And he weeps with us in that place, and does not leave us there. As you go through this process to name and memorialize your baby, be encouraged. See Jesus is with you. Know his love is reflected in the resurrected heart of your child. Know your child has nothing but love for you. Reisser explains:

> No one who's been dwelling in the presence of God lacks an understanding. That aborted child at this point in time feels nothing but absolute and utter compassion for the extreme pressure and immature naiveté that brought you to a place where you felt that you were backed into a corner and could choose nothing but an abortion. Your child has long ago wiped all that off the chart and longs to get to know you, has nothing but love, because that child has God's perspective in his or her heart.[8]

Your child in heaven loves you. This child has the heart of Christ, and this child has known nothing else for the length of his or her life.

Dwell on that. Think how children possessing empathy and care for a parent who has forsaken and abandoned them is a tribute to the powerful love of Jesus. Get the image of that in your mind. Picture a toddler comforting a mother who has stubbed her toe, returning the reassurance he once received. "Don't, cry, Mommy. It's all right." Though we neither gave nor modeled this love to our children, they know it, through Christ because 1 John 3:2 says, "What we [who are children of God] will be has not yet been made known. But we know that when [Jesus] appears, we shall be like him."

This is the purifying hope we have concerning our children right now: in their resurrection, they are already like Jesus, and therefore they love and have forgiven us, just as he loves and has forgiven us. Isn't that amazing? And as Jesus cradles us in his love, he creates in us a pure heart (Ps. 51:10).

Here we stand—pure, loved, forgiven. When we keep our eyes on Jesus and let him lead us through this memorial process, we can come clean in every way. Jesus himself said, "the pure in heart . . . will see God" (Matt. 5:8).

That includes me and it includes you.

Go about good grief

While Jesus heals us through this process, and makes us clean from the inside out, there are outward things that help in the healing too. Just as going to the tomb helped Mary, Martha, and the crowd see Jesus' power, and allowed them to witness Lazarus's new life, there are things you can do to finally lay your baby to rest and celebrate his or her eternal life in heaven.

Ruth said, "Our family portraits include our baby pictures. In the center of the wall of photos hangs an ornately-framed calligraphy in memory of Susan, my child in heaven. 'Let the little children come to me and do not hinder them, for the kingdom of God belongs to such as these' it says, from Mark 10:14. Visitors to my home often remark on the beauty of the colors the artist used in the lettering, and this Scripture has been a wonderful way for me to honor the life of my child and keep her memory alive."

Loving actions toward a deceased child help replace painful memories with loving thoughts. Allow yourself to remember your child and feel love, even though your child is not here to hold. Place a memorial stone in a garden or cemetery. Choose a symbolic way to give life such as planting a tree or placing altar flowers in church in memory of your child. Turn your thoughts toward heaven with a balloon release while saying a simple prayer with a friend who will help you celebrate your hope.

I purchased a gift in Immanuel's honor—a small silver baby cup engraved with his name to display with other family memorabilia and gifts that welcomed children into our family and our hearts. When I see these keepsakes I am reminded how I have been entrusted with the story of my children's lives and I share that story whenever a guest in our home remarks on this special collection. Other women have made a small quilt or crib blanket to use as a wall hanging.

If you have a family tradition, such as giving a special Christmas ornament or keepsake box, you might honor your child's memory with a similar item in his or her name. I also wrote Immanuel a song based on verses from the Psalms. The song helped me feel like Immanuel's mom when I sang it at my group's memorial service.

We all wrote and read simple letters. Mine said I was sorry I had made such a terrible mistake. I asked Immanuel to forgive me and I let him know that I value him, and that I can't wait to see him when at last the Lord will bring us together.

Jesus Calls from the Grave New Life

Ecclesiastes 3:11 says God has made everything beautiful in his time. You may recall that I wondered how the Lord could possibly make beautiful my abominable sin on what for me was the world's worst day.

Because of what I did in taking my Immanuel's life, I never got to see what he might have been, what God had in mind for him. Would he have become a salesman like my dad? Or brainy and funny like my son, Sam? Or artistic and funny like my daughter, Addie? Because of what I did, I'll never know. But I do know this. God saw my child's tiny heart beating within me before I even knew he existed. God knows each of us before we are even born (Isa. 49:1; Jer. 1:5). And my baby's small heart has eternal meaning, because coming to terms with his life and death has made me a follower of Jesus Christ.

What I'm most grateful to Jesus for in this is that, like Mary and Martha and the crowd, he led me to where I had laid Immanuel and then brought forth new life. My baby is at the heart of a new work and purpose: Immanuel's ministry—to help people see the truth in abortion, beginning with me and now extended to you. His story has touched hundreds of lives. Though he only lived for those twelve short weeks within my womb, his spirit and life witness the eternal worth and value of each and every person God has created. He has taught me to love, and to trust, and to hope. I know I will see him in heaven, where the Bible says there will be no tears and where we will be one in Christ.

When I am ever tempted to think only of the grief, an unending mourning, I think on these things and am reminded that this is how God has fulfilled his promise to me to make all things beautiful in his time. The story of the life and death of my child who lives on in heaven has become the story of the beauty of God's merciful redeeming love.

That beauty and new life and hope can be yours too. The apostle Paul said, "Brothers, we do not want you to be ignorant about those who fall asleep [in other words, die], or to grieve like the rest of men, who have no hope. . . . We will be with the Lord forever. Therefore encourage each other with these words" (1 Thess. 4:13, 17–18).

Sharing our stories, memorializing our babies together is how we grieve like God but not "like the rest of men." Bible commentator Matthew Henry explains that comfort in this way:

> Death is an unknown thing, and we know little about the state after death; yet the doctrines of the resurrection and the second coming of Christ, are a remedy against the fear of death, and undue sorrow. . . . It will be some happiness that all the saints shall meet, and remain together for ever; but the principal happiness of heaven is to be with the Lord, to see him, live with him, and enjoy him for ever. We should support one another in times of sorrow; not deaden one another's spirits, or weaken one another's hands. And this may be done by the many lessons to be learned from the resurrection of the dead, and the second coming of Christ.[9]

Abortion cannot diminish our hearts as mothers and fathers unless we allow ourselves to grieve endlessly without hope. Jesus, our bridge of heavenly hope, shows us how to grieve and memorialize and then love the new life that he calls forth. As he did for Mary and Martha and

Lazarus and the crowd that day at the tomb where his friend had been lain, he enlarges our hearts toward all children everywhere.

Psalm 40:1–3 says the Lord hears our cries. He lifts us out of the mire of grief and gives us a new song. He did that for me, and I wrote this song for all my children, inspired by Immanuel, my child in heaven:

Morning Lullaby

As high as the heavens are above the earth,
Ocean wide, deep, dark and blue;
Up to the moon and the stars and the sun and back again,
So great is my love for you.
As new as the morning light that dawns each day,
Riding in on the wings of the wind;
Such is the love from the Father's hand as he formed your heart,
Ever true, faithful and free.
   Bridge:
   It's not a song 'til someone hears you singing,
   It's not a gift 'til someone will receive,
   Yet hearts before they're born are known in heaven,
   For he made each one and loves us sight unseen.
As high as the heavens are above the earth,
Ocean wide, deep, dark and blue;
Up to the moon and the stars and the sun and back again,
So great is my love for you,
So great is God's love for you,
So great is my love for you.

So great is Christ's love for us. Keep your eyes fixed on him and he will lead you to where you've buried, but not laid to rest, your grief for your baby.

He will give you a new purity and love and forgiveness. And as he shows you the new life he's given your child and you, he will give you, too, a new song.

—— *Reflect* ——————————————————

Read for yourself in John 11 about Jesus' miracle in raising Lazarus from the dead. Notice Jesus says his sickness and death was meant to glorify God (John 11:4), just as Jesus once said a man born blind was meant for the glory of God (John 9:3). As you read the story of Lazarus, note how many times faith and belief are mentioned in the story. Pray for the gift of faith to believe the truth of this historic account as you also think upon these Bible promises:

- "Even though I walk through the valley of the shadow of death, I will fear no evil, for you are with me" (Ps. 23:4).
- "He gathers the lambs in his arms and carries them close to his heart" (Isa. 40:11).
- Resurrection is reality: "For what I received I passed on to you as of first importance: that Christ died for our sins . . . , that he was buried, that he was raised on the third day . . . , that he appeared to Peter, and then to the Twelve. After that, he appeared to more than five hundred of the brothers at the same time. . . . Then he appeared to James, then to all the apostles, and . . . he appeared to me also, as to one abnormally born" (1 Cor. 15:3–8).
- Restoration brings rejoicing: "You turned my wailing into dancing; you removed my sackcloth and clothed me with joy, that my heart may sing to you and not be silent. O LORD my God, I will give you thanks forever" (Ps. 30:11–12).
- "But because of his great love for us, God, who is rich in mercy, made us alive with Christ even when we were dead in transgressions—it is by grace you have been saved" (Eph. 2:4–5).
- "I write these things to you who believe in the name of the Son of God so that you may know that you have eternal life. This is the confidence we have in approaching God: that if we ask anything according to his will, he hears us. And if we know that he hears us—whatever we ask—we know that we have what we asked of him" (1 John 5:13–15).

Request

Lord, before you formed me in my mother's womb, you knew me and you knew my unborn child. I humbly ask that you would grant me spiritual knowledge of this child so that I may give my baby a name. Help me in this task of giving honor and dignity to the child of mine whom you have so lovingly received in heaven. Help me, Lord, to grieve with hope. In Jesus' name, I pray. Amen.

Respond

- Make the decision this week to seek the support of a postabortion Bible study or healing support group. Some groups meet weekly, others offer a weekend retreat format, prayer vigils, and local or national groups that Walk for Life. Check appendix A and connect with those who can help you begin to formally grieve. Don't pressure yourself to leave your sadness behind all at once. Start small with a phone call to explore whether a particular program is right for you: How large is the group? Where are the meetings held? How much time will be required to complete the group? Is there a cost? What else can you expect to experience?
- Grieving with hope means sharing your heart as you move out of isolation and despair. As a way to start honoring the memory of your child, let someone know about the new perspective you are gaining on heaven. It may not be wise to share your full story with everyone, but start some conversations to share the blessed hope God gives of heaven and to share Jesus, our bridge of hope. You may be surprised how many others have been nurturing the hurt of child loss due to abortion or miscarriage and how much caring others have to offer.
- List the ways your family welcomes the birth of new children and consider taking one such action to express caring toward your child in heaven—it could be as simple as a special memorial gift that you add without comment to your regular offering next Sunday at church. If you like to write poetry or letters, write to your child. For less than a dollar you can purchase or make a pretty bookmark to tuck into your Bible to remind you of your

little one with thoughts of love and joy. If you find God's love in the beauty of nature, select a spot in your garden or a park to purchase a bench or plant a tree. These caring gestures need not be explained to everyone; exercise discernment as you bring others into this circle of love and as God's Spirit leads.

- Sponsor a plaque or monument at the National Memorial for the Unborn in Chattanooga, Tennessee, dedicated to the memory of unborn children, particularly those lost in abortion (www.memorialfortheunborn.org). Online memorials allow you to share a tribute and read what others have written to their loved ones who have died.

- Listen to these songs to help you keep your eyes on Jesus just as Mary and Martha learned to do as they both grieved the loss of their brother and then celebrated his new life. Sing them this week: "In His Time" by Diane Ball, "Because He Lives" by Bill and Gloria Gaither, and "You Never Let Go" by Matt Redman. Jesus is at hand to see us through our grief. "Christ Is Risen" by Matt Maher and Mia Fieldes celebrates the miraculous truth that Jesus defeated death by death, and "Just a Closer Walk with Thee," the traditional hymn as sung by Mahalia Jackson, is an uplifting look ahead to being with God in heaven.

- The film *Sarah's Choice* with Rebecca St. James follows one woman's decisions through pregnancy, and features a moving and poignant memorial for a child lost to abortion.

A Dedication

Will you rise again?

As you begin to heal from abortion's scars, you may also begin to grasp Jesus' plan to love you so well you will want to live his way. And yet, you still will wonder if others will accept you once they know about your past. You may feel disqualified from serving as a leader—or even serving at all—marked by the blemish of bad choices. But rather than marking you as unfit, your hard-won faith equips you to bring hope about abortion to this world, beginning right at home, and your love is what makes restoration complete.

I learned this en route to volunteer as the emcee for an event promoting equality for women and girls. *I would take a bullet for you, Lord,* I thought as I was driving.

Opportunities to be in the spotlight had come often in my previous twenty-five years in broadcasting. But the blessing of a new powder blue suit made this night seem extra special, as if God were saying, *Look and feel good about this because I am redeeming the career you once chose over your child by allowing you to give witness about the love of Jesus Christ in your community.* For years I'd feared disclosing my past. I had so much to lose: respect, value. *What would people think of me?* But my fears had proved unfounded. Thus far, people had responded warmly to my honesty, my ignited faith, my story.

So I drove to the event, feeling encouraged and equipped, ready to shine where God was planting me. I flipped on the radio and listened to a story about a country where Christianity is forbidden by law. Immediately I was mesmerized as the radio host told about a family dragged outside their home by armed soldiers who made the ten-year-old son kneel before his parents and younger siblings. With a gun jammed to the boy's temple, the soldiers demanded the father renounce Jesus Christ. But before the father could answer, the boy cried, "I will never renounce Jesus!"

He was shot dead.

The soldiers then forced the father to watch as they shot his wife and the rest of his children before they took him into custody. The father's faith in God never faltered. He remained steadfast, and when eventually freed by the government, he began preaching the meaning of the life and death of Jesus worldwide by sharing the story of his family's courage and faith.

The radio host noted Americans are rich in both God's material blessings and the freedom to openly practice faith. He warned we should never pervert the message of being "rich in Christ" in light of the fact that people are still being martyred for proclaiming the gospel message today.

I turned off the radio feeling humbled and even more grateful to God for my new spiritual freedom in Christ. I thought how moments earlier I'd given God credit for my material prosperity because of my new suit. *But,* I wondered, *how would I react if I was forced to put my faith on the line to save my family?*

I was surprised. For the first time in my life I actually felt confident that I could stand up for my faith. This newfound willingness in my heart to give my life for my faith was a significant step forward. Was God exchanging a new courage for the cowardice I demonstrated on the day my child had died?

I had publicly laid down my reputation in sharing the truth about abortion, and now here I was, still standing after all.

And so I arrived at the event. As we were being seated, I heard the announcement, "Watch the screens." A rotating roster of community organizations that would benefit from the proceeds of this year's event streamed before everyone's eyes. "Give generously," the announcement continued. I took my seat as one of the slides in particular caught my eye and then took my breath away. The name and a photo of the entrance of the abortion facility where I had taken the life of my child twenty-four years earlier had just flashed on the screen!

During the years I'd languished in denial, I had lost most of my memory of that place. I could remember the general location of the abortion facility I'd gone to, but I couldn't remember the name—and I wanted to remember it, for the sake of telling others the whole story of how far into the darkness Jesus had gone to bring me back to the light of truth. I'd considered driving by, just to see, but feared it would be too painful and sad to return to the scene of my child's death and the failure of my will.

Now, here it was, right in front of me, the name of that facility splashed across a screen. I sat riveted. The room around me seemed to fade as my eyes fixed on the next slide. A woman in a white lab coat and a young woman sat smiling at each other across a desk. A wave of nausea swept over me as I conjured the full ugliness of the transaction behind that pretty picture. I knew what took place behind those doors.

The next thing I heard was, "And now, please welcome Kim Jeffries."

I knew I needed to get up and walk to the front of the room, fully aware that my participation in this event would benefit and advance my mortal enemy—the facility and staff who helped to end my child's life. My work this night would put money into their hands. My work would further their cause. Somehow, by simple reflex, at the sound of my professional name, I stood and went forward.

And I failed to utter a word against that place of death and destruction in my life.

The event seemed to last forever. I held myself together by smiling and falling into a professional geniality, and my hollow pledge of courage from a few scant hours earlier mocked me with growing intensity as the evening wore on. All I could think of was how eager I was for the moment when I could escape to the safety of my car. When at last I could, I went outside and wept bitterly, praying for Jesus to help me avoid ever disowning him like that again.

I had pledged to tell of his love. Instead, I'd participated in a fundraiser to further abortion, death, and lies.

Could Jesus ever place his trust in me again? Was I really equipped to not only live but give, in service, this new life?

Mistakes Are a Stumble, Not a Loss of Faith

I had only to turn to Luke 22:14–34 to get an answer. My experience was Simon Peter's too. Just before Jesus' death, Peter also faced such an evening like each of us encounter once we've chosen new life. For Peter, as for me, this happened at a dinner.

At the Last Supper with his inner circle, Jesus altered the Passover ritual by declaring his kingdom was at hand—one in which new life starts from within and is realized through grace. New life wasn't going to be any easier, he was saying, but it would be lighter because it required not a series of works but a belief in his grace. Believe in that grace, he was telling Peter, as he warned of a great test of faith that was coming Peter's way. But Peter dismissed the warning.

"Lord, I'm ready to go with you to prison and to death," Peter insisted (v. 33). He thought his will alone could forge the way into this new life.

Jesus knew otherwise. "Before the rooster crows today, you will deny three times that you know me," he told Peter (v. 34). Jesus then asked Peter to watch and pray during his anguish in Gethsemane (Mark 14:32–42), even though he knew Peter would fail this test.

Prayer will get you through the tests

But Jesus said falling asleep on the job is not the ultimate test of faith. There would be greater tests, and prayer would get you through each one—because will alone is not enough. "The spirit is willing, but the body is weak" (Mark 14:38), Jesus said to Peter; in other words, *You are only human, and subject to weakness.* He also was saying we should understand and expect that tests of our faith will come once we've chosen new life.

"Simon, Simon," he warned Peter, "Satan has asked to sift you as wheat. But I have prayed for you, Simon, that your faith may not fail. And when you have turned back, strengthen your brothers" (Luke 22:31–32).

I have prayed for you.
That your faith may not fail.
Such powerful words.

Jesus prays for us

The idea is stunning, actually, that Christ prays for each of us to face every test of faith. The Savior of the world, the Lord, the one who created you and knows you (every good and bad thing you've done), prays for you. He believes in you. He's rooting for you. He knows when we can take the bullet—when it will result in his greater glory. He knows we can defy the attacks to our faith, just as the man who summoned extraordinary courage to witness after watching his family die for Christ, just as Peter pledged to do, just as I could have done, standing up for him at that dinner.

Living restored takes more than will

But defying the attacks on faith takes more than will. Knowing we can lose the will without having to lose faith makes all the difference. An athlete can miss several shots but still win the game. Our will may be weak in the face of a test, yet our faith can be strengthened by failing that test. A failure of will may lead us into sin, but that is never as serious as a failure of faith which can threaten to lead us straight to hell. Where Satan constantly attacks our will, God never tempts us to do evil (James 1:13). He provides us with many tests from time to time to know where we are heading in the development of both our will to obey him (Deut. 8:2) and our love for him (Job 1:6–12). But he believes in us. Jesus prays for us.

The key to understanding this is the idea Jesus uses of Satan wanting to "sift" us.

You will be sifted like wheat

Sifting wheat on a farm involves threshing by spreading the wheat grains on a hard surface floor and beating or flailing them with sharp instruments. Sometimes animals tread or trample the grain to separate the wheat from the chaff, which is the grain's outer covering. The grain is what's wanted. The chaff, which has no value except in recycling, is then swept or blown away.

By allowing Satan to sift us, God obtains what he wants from us spiritually, eliminating whatever is of no value. He wants our total trust in him, complete faith—and he wants for us to know our own hearts so we can begin to trust in dependence on him and not on our own strength. Jesus summed this up for the apostle Paul by saying, "My grace is sufficient for you, for my power is made perfect in weakness" (2 Cor. 12:9).

The entire book of Job is a story of sifting and faith.[1] Job endures much and God shows him in the end that keeping faith is what matters, that loving God as much as he loves us is what he wants. Sifting accurately, and often painfully, reflects to us the state of our faith by forcing us to act upon how much we really know, love, and trust God. But it's as much for us as for him. Sifting helps us settle the matter of our actual relationship with God once and for all in our own hearts. Are we giving to God just to get blessings back? Are we obeying with reservations, planning to move on to our true desires afterward? Are we simply hoping for a different outcome than the perfect plan God has always had in mind for us—do we give him the ultimate right to decide what's best for us? Sifting may feel like a beating, a flailing, a trampling. Really, though, it is a purifying and through it, just as he reassured Peter, Jesus always prays for us, so we may help others learn to love God by faithful actions that reflect God's love.

For Peter, the test was painful as both a follower and a leader. He had caught the vision of Jesus as Messiah, the promised king. But when he saw his leader and his hope being willingly led away by the Roman authorities, he fell. He tried first to fight for faith. He cut off the ear of one of Jesus' captors (John 18:10). Then, even as Jesus' hand-picked successor, the one on whom Christ said he would build the church, things got even worse.

One Last Look

Jesus was led across a courtyard to begin the process of his trial and torture. Peter was there to see Jesus being led. Instead of stepping forward, however, or even following, Peter stayed put on the sidelines. He voiced his denials to three different people, mostly bystanders in the crowd. When Jesus overheard the third denial, apparently made behind his back, he turned around and looked straight at Peter. Those denials were the last words Jesus would hear Peter speak in this, their final encounter before he was to die (Luke 22:54–62).

What do you suppose Jesus' look said? Surprise? He had predicted Peter would deny him. Anger? He had warned Peter to watch for a sifting, a test. Disappointment? But he had put his trust in Peter, saying upon Peter he would build the church, and that he would be praying for him.

Instead, no words were exchanged. The only sound recorded was that of the cock crowing, the very signal Christ had foretold.

Jesus had known Peter's heart would fail him. Jesus had always known Peter's heart. So perhaps that last look he gave Peter matched the expression of another last goodbye, the one sealed by his betrayer's fatal kiss in the garden (Matt. 26:49). Perhaps it was a look of love; for Peter's failure of faith in that moment did not exceed the power of Jesus' love. Perhaps it was a look that simply said, "Peter, my friend, I love you."

Such a look can transform you.

Such a look transformed a young woman much like Peter. Bonnie grew up in a very strong pro-life family, but she became sexually active with boys her own age after abuse from a trusted adult.

She became pregnant and chose, rather than tell her parents, to have an abortion. "I had decided rather than put my family through the shame, I will go to hell," she explains.

A woman at the clinic sensed Bonnie was struggling with her decision.

"I told her my dad and I had both been very active serving at our church which taught against abortion," Bonnie says, "and so going through with it was really hard for me. She looked at me and said, 'Well, you won't be doing that anymore, will you now?'"

The question captured the sifting Bonnie would go through the remainder of her schooling and young adulthood as a result of her abortion when she was a teen. Her faith had taught her that abortion was wrong, but she couldn't face the truth with her parents. She'd disappointed them—and herself.

But Jesus loved her anyway, she learned. Only she had trouble truly trusting that his suffering and death was enough to restore her relationship with God. The sifting continued: trust in what she thought might save her, continuing to fight for faith and prove her love—or rest in Christ's.

When Bonnie finally found the courage to return to church and tell her friends there about her abortion, she was surprised so many other women suffered under the same mistake. When she then told her family, they were devastated, but accepting. Their love won her over, showing her how Christ loves us whether we fail or fly through a sifting. Christ wants the valuable part of us, the soul, and he is willing to wait through the sifting to get it.

Today, Bonnie and her dad once more stand tall for the cause of life as they worship in church together. "My dad is so proud of me, and he sees me for who I really am," Bonnie says. "He is able to see so much good in me that is only there because of my faith. He recently looked at me and said, 'You will help restore others and protect innocent life. You can do it because you've been through it."

The Dedicated Life

That is the beautiful thing about sifting. It gets to the core of you, allows you to share all you've been through in order for people to see Christ reflected and for him to redeem others.

Getting there, the sifting process itself, is not easy though. It must have been agony for Peter to have lived with the knowledge of his failure while Jesus lay in the tomb. Peter's own words must have echoed in his heart, "I don't know him!" (Luke 22:57).

Imagine, then, Peter's ecstasy over the glorious news that Jesus had risen from the dead, and the tomb was empty!

Such a powerful thing.

As if that were not enough—so that Peter would know that his failure did not mean he was unable to serve and dedicate himself to a new life, Jesus had a private conversation with Peter when all the men were out fishing early one morning. And what do you think that conversation was about? A reprimand for Peter's denials of him? An "I told you so"?

No, it was a conversation about love (John 21:15–17).

"Do you love me?" Jesus asked Peter. Three times, he asked, "Do you love me?"

The answer created a new sound in Peter's ear to replace the sound of the cock crowing three times, and the bitter tears he had shed after hearing his own denials.

To each of the Lord's questions in this conversation, Peter told Jesus, "Lord, you know I love you." Understandably, Peter was hurt because Jesus asked him the third time.

How much we are like Peter. When we fall short, and Jesus returns to ask us, "Do you love me?" the hurt is meant to reveal our deepest deception about ourselves—mistaken notions about God's call on our lives, our own capabilities, or the very things we have believed, placed faith in, or built our lives around.

But when we look at the Lord instead of ourselves and our deceptions, we see Christ's love. We see ourselves in his light. We see love—his love for us and our love for him—and then we are ready to strengthen others in faith with the story of our fall and his restoration.

Love was the only qualification Peter would ever need to be Jesus' friend, a friend to others, and God's man among Jesus' followers. Jesus' questioning served as a lifelong reminder to Peter about what the motivation of his faith should be: love, not a proving of his own worth. Jesus wants our love to make a difference in the world.

There is such a temptation to try to repair our image after we fail. Feeling we have utterly lost face, we may adopt a permanent mask to cover the shame. But Jesus wants all self-confidence to be stripped away so his love can dominate our hearts. Jesus didn't call us to be self-confident or perfect—he calls us to be his. Peter's failure and restoration can help us grasp the ultimate purpose of the calling to love and serve Christ.

TIMELESS TRUTH
Jesus didn't call us to be perfect—he calls us to be his.

Peter's sifting, and mine, offer encouragement that every mistake we make, every sifting we go through, can be redeemed when we share the story with others. In times of sifting, remember these important truths . . .

Relationship is everything

You have a secure place in God's family through faith (1 John 3:1). When you falter, it's all part of being in his family and experiencing his perfect love. Sometimes you're shown the limits of your love so you can know where God wants you to grow.

Chastening is to be expected—and welcomed

Failures are God's teachable moments. Peter learned the importance of prayer after he saw the result of his fatigue that night in Gethsemane. Likewise, Jesus chastens, as he did when Peter cut off a soldier's ear, when you try to accomplish spiritual work within your own power. It's what he did for me when I took confidence in wearing that powder blue suit instead of in wearing the grace of Christ. I overestimated my spiritual capacity and underestimated my weak flesh. I disowned Jesus with my stunned silence. For all I know, a child's life may have been on the line that night. There may have been someone in that room thinking about an abortion. There may have been someone who saw the smiling people in the slides and thought abortion was a good option. There may have been someone who could have been spared from making a deadly choice.

To think silence doesn't affect others is to fool ourselves. Children are dying from abortion every day due to silence and neglect. *U.S. News and World Report* notes that the 2009 Annual Report of Planned Parenthood, one of our nation's largest abortion providers, listed 324,008 abortions performed in their facilities that year alone.[2] The precision of the number is a chilling reminder that abortion as public policy carries a body count.

God's chastening helped me see my weakness. God always knows and forgives just how weak we are apart from him (Ps. 103:13–14). I had a new suit but I wasn't prepared to put on the full armor of God (see Eph. 6:10–20) in the battle for hearts and lives.

The Holy Spirit will help you

Faith not only takes its time to be prepared, but needs God's help through the indwelling of the Holy Spirit, who empowers each of us to operate in God's power. Peter learned to pray through the temptations to rest too early in battle or to shrink back from the crowd.

These testing moments let you count the cost of standing with Jesus when the pressure is great. Pray whenever God gives you the chance to speak in front of others, even if it's just family and friends. Speak his Word, and allow it to work in the hearts of those who hear, without arguing or strife. Trust God's Word to do God's work. He has promised, "My word that goes out from my mouth . . . will not return to me empty, but will accomplish what I desire and achieve the purpose for which I sent it" (Isa. 55:11).

Since the night of my sifting, whenever I have the microphone, I pray to know how to be prepared. The Spirit has helped me, just as Jesus promised, showing me there are simple, strong, gracious ways to respond. On that night I could have said simply, "I see you're being asked to support [this organization]. I hope you will 'choose life.'" This would have been speaking God's Word (Deut. 30:19) and standing on truth.

Your worst failure can be God's greatest redemption

Peter thought his faith was rock solid at the Last Supper, when Jesus spoke of his mission. Maybe you thought something similar in a situation where you've had the chance to tell your family and friends the truth about abortion. But you remained silent, maybe out of fear, or self-preservation, or other anxious thoughts. Be encouraged. Peter failed at what Jesus called the ultimate test of love—he did not lay down his life for his friend (John 15:13). Yet, Jesus restored Peter and empowered him to stand strong for God's truth as he became the leader the Lord had always intended him to be, a leader just as flawed and frail as the rest of us are at times.

Abortion may have represented a failure of our faith, but the renewal of our hope can also provide a way back to God for others whose hearts are broken. God never wastes a hurt. In offering others true hope, our healing is complete.

When Jesus healed the sliced-off ear of the soldier in the garden during his arrest, he was restraining Peter from defending him at the wrong time and in the wrong way.

He urges us to beware of defending him at the wrong time in the wrong way. As women restored after choosing abortion, he doesn't want us to rush in with swords to defend the truth about life. He doesn't want us to look at people with surprise or anger or disappointment, but with love. He wants us to take time to pray, and to seek the counsel of a mature believer who can prayerfully support when and with whom you will share your story. He wants us to be prepared.

It's All About Love

Peter was not the only one of his followers who failed Jesus. Like Judas, you may continue to suffer over having betrayed your faith when you chose abortion. What a portrait of worldly sorrow, for Judas ultimately chose to take his life, showing the difference between repentance and remorse.

He let his pride, rather than love for Jesus, guide him. Instead of going to the ones who held Jesus hostage and admitting his mistake, Judas tragically tried to correct his own wrong, looking for validation in the wrong place. He tried to return the money to those who had paid him, but they treated him with brutal indifference and laid the sole responsibility on his shoulders.

What a stark contrast to the kindness Jesus had shown him the night before, when Jesus withstood Judas's deadly kiss and called him, "friend" (Matt. 26:50).

God doesn't want you to make the same mistake. He is always kind to lead us back to his love (Rom. 2:4). Judas couldn't go there. He knew he was wrong, but by attempting to return the money, he sought solace from the ones who had led him into evil, trying to make things right on his own instead of turning to God for forgiveness.

You and I can make another choice. We need not return for solace from the defenders of abortion in our culture, those who refuse to acknowledge any damage done to women and families. Their attitude seems to be, "It was your choice. You deal with all the consequences."

In my ignorance of Jesus' character, that is what I feared from God and godly people for all those years of anguish and heartache. I was so blinded by my pain that I feared God would throw me away and say as the priests and elders did to Judas in Matthew 27:4, *What is that to me?*

Instead, God looked at me like Jesus looked at Peter—with love.

God never answers a simple, heartfelt, and sincere confession any other way. He says of his servant, Jesus, "A bruised reed he will not break, and a smoldering wick he will not snuff out" (Isa. 42:3). These words mean that God has already exacted every punishment for every sin from Jesus on our behalf.

The Lord wants everyone to come to repentance, to live fully restored (2 Peter 3:9). Without question, Peter failed Jesus on that terrible night. The margin of victory for Peter versus Judas, however, was Peter's love. And the prayer of Jesus that Peter's faith would not fail (Luke 22:32). A broken heart over having hurt Jesus produced godly sorrow that left Peter room for hope.

His love makes a difference. Peter's love for Jesus would give him the courage he needed to fulfill his assignment to love and nurture the people God would entrust into his care.

You are blessed to be a blessing

In the years following my powder blue defeat, God has made me bold to stand for truth in the public square when it comes to abortion. I'm no longer associated with the professional name and brand I built at the expense of my family and faith.

My faith now is in Jesus Christ and his plan for my life—a safe place of rest from all the disasters of a self-reliant lifestyle. How I wish I had known the Lord and been able to seek his guidance as I made relationship choices as a young woman, especially when I married my first husband. Our chance of success was greatly limited since I did not have the love of Jesus Christ at the center of my vow, and I was still suffering from the loss of my first child. I achieved my goal of motherhood and for that I thank God, but my children suffered from my ignorance of God and lack of faith, especially as I divorced and remarried a few years later. Yet God has been so gracious to bless my children with faith. He has seen them through to adulthood despite my many shortcomings. In their teenage years I told them the truth about my abortion experience, and we've worked through the pain of that to find our peace. I told them I had made a horrible mistake—and that I'm not who I was when I chose that awful act. I reassured them of my love.

I have fully repented of my former attitudes about marriage and family, and I am proud to carry my husband's name. As we now approach our twentieth anniversary, our marriage is founded on Christ and serving him together.

You can share at home

In his time I've learned God's plan was for me first to tell the truth about my experience with everyone in my family. My parents gave their blessing to my ministry of truth about abortion. They are now both deceased, and I wish that I had sought their love and support so much sooner.

You can serve God after abortion by being a faithful servant in your family. If we are married we can endeavor to truly become one in Christ, each one letting Jesus lead us as we maintain our individuality in a way that helps us put each other first. God has graced me to learn this and live this with my husband, Bruce. We lean on Jesus and not each other, we seek his will and not our own, and we agree to agree with Jesus and his ways in all things. Following God's pattern has allowed me to find appropriate expressions of parental and step-parental love. I've come to see we honor our living children best when we accept them exactly for who they are, something that may prove very difficult to do unless we have been healed from betraying another child by abortion. Perfectionism, overprotection, and other anguish over our kids' emotional well-being are parenting red flags which may signal trying to atone for an abortion in your past. We learn healthy relationships as we develop our new life in faith within the support of our community of faith.

Sharing away from home

Proclaiming the truth about abortion as child death is primarily a spiritual act of faith. If the Lord prompts you to publicly defend God's truth and protect the children through political action or public discourse, I pray you will be bold to obey. You and I have a vital role to play in winning the hearts and minds of those who don't understand the human cost of abortion. Let's live up to the first call of spiritual activism—knowing Jesus and making his cause known. Our witness may save lives.

When God asks you to risk something in order to share the truth, it is always for the benefit of others. Oswald Chambers says that we don't get to choose the place of our martyrdom.[3] Dying to self is not the spiritual suicide Judas resorted to when he refused to submit to the mercy of Christ. Instead, we are to meet every call to sacrifice and speak the truth with joy for all the Lord has given us. We have this new life now. And we look forward in hope to the promise of the life to come. Our actions may betray our faith, and yes, we may deny him. But Jesus will never allow our sincere faith to utterly fail us. He uses our witness to a spiritually lost and dying world. We are blessed to be that blessing. Peter's failure is not the end of the story, of course. He went on to build the early church as God sent the Holy Spirit to empower his ministry and his new life in Christ.

God's love knows no limits—our failures do not constrain his holy purpose for our lives. We can still love the Lord with all of our hearts, souls, minds, and strength. We can dedicate ourselves to him and his purposes. As he gives us the chance to share his love with others, we will find he has plans for us we never could have dreamed.

God always writes the best endings.

—— *Reflect* ————————————————————————————

Read for yourself in Luke 22:7–62 the story of one of Peter's heartrending encounters with Jesus, followed by John 20–21 about Peter's restoration. Notice Jesus' final words in the Gospels are spoken to Peter, who still required instruction from his loving Lord and teacher. Spend time reading the rest of the story in the book of Acts to learn how Peter moved in power once he was filled with the Holy Spirit. Now think upon these passages:

- "'Love the Lord your God with all your heart and with all your soul and with all your mind.' This is the first and greatest commandment. And the second is like it: 'Love your neighbor as yourself'" (Matt. 22:37–39).
- "Love never fails" (1 Cor. 13:8).
- "Speak up for those who cannot speak for themselves" (Prov. 31:8).
- "If anyone would come after me, he must deny himself and take up his cross daily and follow me. For whoever wants to save his life will lose it, but whoever loses his life for me will save it. What good is it for a man to gain the whole world, and yet lose or forfeit his very self? If anyone is ashamed of me and my words, the Son of Man will be ashamed of him when he comes in his glory and in the glory of the Father and of the holy angels" (Luke 9:23–26).
- "Do nothing out of selfish ambition or vain conceit, but in humility consider others better than yourselves. Each of you should look not only to your own interests, but also to the interests of others" (Phil. 2:3–4).

—— *Request* ————————————————————

Lord, help me live up to my faith in grateful appreciation for my new life now. Help me make my life one of praise and thankfulness in all things. I ask for you to work any and all changes in my heart that you desire in order to make me who you want me to be, in Jesus' name. Amen.

—— *Respond* ————————————————————

- Think about who needs to know of your abortion and why. Pray about this, and as you do, call on people to support you to help you think through the decision to share your experience with others. Here are some dos and don'ts to consider:

  Do take your time—wait until your spirit is at peace before sharing your story with others.

  Do take care—realize that knowledge of abortion may be upsetting to young children. Make sure such conversations are necessary and age-appropriate.

Do listen—an emotional reaction may or may not occur, so be prepared to offer your support.

Don't force yourself to share with someone who has not earned your trust.

Don't worry about winning the opinions of those who don't understand your faith; pray for them.

Don't go it alone. If you feel you must have a conversation with someone who is likely to become angry or unkind, take a friend along for support.

- Put your faith on the line in some small way this week; behind closed doors, commit to pray for someone new. With friends and family, offer to pray for someone who confides something in you, or pause for a prayer before meals. Choose a piece of jewelry or clothing to express your faith in Jesus Christ. A simple cross necklace is one clear way to declare your faith; wearing a pin shaped like a butterfly symbolizes new life; a charm with the name of your child in heaven could start a conversation in a gentle, nonconfrontational way. Wear your "Sunday best" clothes on a day other than Sunday to remind yourself to offer God your best that day. If others remark on your jewelry or apparel, tell them of your desire to be dedicated to the Lord.

- Be sensitive to the opportunities God provides to share the love you've found in Jesus, and the truth about abortion, asking God to show you favor as these occasions arise. For example, when someone brings up the topic of pregnancy loss or abortion, ask if that person knows anyone who has gone through it—you may then sense a chance to share your story. You may also start a conversation by mentioning something not directly related to abortion you may have learned while reading this book. Realize you can witness your new view without disclosing your whole story.

- Be wise with family and friends who may oppose your new thoughts about abortion or who may be unable or unwilling to forgive you. Abuse may begin or increase due to angry feelings about being excluded from such an important decision. Likewise, if someone coerced you, that person may fear being exposed, and they may try to discredit your story or prevent you from speaking out. Family difficulties can arise over sharing the truth with your children who are not yet fully prepared to receive it; they have lost a sibling they never knew existed. Seek support to uphold your new life in Christ before you proceed to share God's truth with others, and lean on this support throughout the process of the decision to tell your story to others. As a rule of thumb, do not share your story with a loved one to take care of your spiritual and emotional needs. Try your best to see to it that you are cared for and nurtured in your faith first so you can begin to offer nurturing to others.

- Listen or sing along to songs that help motivate you to tell others of the power of God's love in your life: "By Our Love" by Christy Nockles says we'll be known by our love as we reach out to offer God's comfort. "Not Ashamed" by the Newsboys is an encouragement that we need not hide our faith to please people. Read the lyrics in a hymnal for "Take My Life and Let It Be" by Frances Havergal, expressing the yielded heart's desire to please God at all times and in every way. "Testify" by Avalon is a song of the joy of shouting God's praises as a witness to God's love.

A Celebration

What would you give out of love?

Having faith in the audacious promise of Jesus Christ and his resurrection allows us to encounter his love after abortion, just as the encounters with Jesus Christ led to healing for each person he touched during his earthly ministry. In every case, as with us, Jesus never healed a person at someone else's expense.

With God, no one is ignored for the sake of another, and so after abortion, God has not forgotten the children. Neither should we.

Restitution toward those we have harmed is God's practical, yet radical plan to establish us in good standing with our children and our world. As we celebrate our new life after abortion, we are called to exercise justice in the here and now by paying back what was never ours to take.

As an act of love and gratitude, what else could we possibly give God in return?

Picture a Heart Overflowing

The taxman's chief of staff arrived in his office out of breath and agitated, announcing, "The governor-elect is on his way to the capitol, Sir. He should be on Main Street in minutes."

It was way too early in the day for this. Rumors had been circulating for weeks that the new man planned to pass through their little outpost of a town the morning of his inauguration. The taxman kept saying, "I'll believe it when I see it!"

Now the aide continued, "Sir, the crowds are whipped up like I have never seen. Word is this governor means to radically change things here with pardons and reforms. And they love this guy."

The taxman was a reviled and hated villain whose lust for the good life had led him to abuse his own people while carrying out the government agenda of shakedowns and other strong-arm tactics to collect the unfair tax, along with other acts of extortion. For years he had taken his cut, funneling money from the town's poorest people into his own pocket. And the richer he got, the less ground the poor could gain to oppose him by the force of law. His corruption made him appear invincible, thus he was despised. And there was no oversight—no one really cared how he ran his ship. His policies ensured just enough unrest, and the occasional riot, to cement his image as guardian of the public safety. The law-and-order crowd at the capitol backed him. The politicians gave him a free hand just as long as they got theirs. He used and abused that power to break down doors, seize property, even to take children as conscription to pay the exorbitant tax.

"You know what?" he said to his aide. "I'd love to meet this guy—let's hit the street!"

He hoped the crowd would make a show of force so he could demonstrate how he and his henchmen were needed to keep the peace.

"All hands!" he ordered as his staff of enforcers took their places to garrison him on the sidewalk.

The general frenzy set the stage for the mayhem the taxman felt sure would ensue. There was just one thing he hadn't counted on that day.

The noise level indicated the governor had arrived. The taxman stepped outside. Instead of the angry mob he expected, the people made the governor's arrival seem like a ticker-tape parade. Cheering and smiling, their high-fives and fist bumps showered the new man with praise. People looked downright jubilant. Their whistles sounded distinctly different from the hostile catcalls and growls they normally voiced for government officials. As he listened, he realized that he was hearing something new. It was joy. And it was astounding. Hundreds of men together reached out to pat the governor on the back or shake his hand. The taxman almost forgot who these guys were as he clambered up a boulevard tree above them to better observe the scene. Suddenly two of the locals moved low to tackle the governor, and a couple of the taxman's thugs stepped forward from the wall where they'd been ordered to wait, but the taxman signaled his guards to stand down.

The two men suddenly scooped up the governor and hoisted him onto their shoulders. They began to parade him around the crowd. The noise grew louder and more joyous—in part because the governor so obviously loved receiving their praise! His charisma was utterly contagious, and now the locals seemed to cheer in one voice. Their energy was magnetic. As the men carried the laughing governor his way, the taxman even smiled and gave a nod.

"Jim! Good to see you!" the governor said, smiling back. "Come down here—I have to stay at your place today."

Some in the crowd suddenly fell silent, though the cheering lingered. Before they could react, the governor disappeared into the inner sanctum of the taxman's office.

"We should have known he was one of theirs," one townsman muttered as the others started to shuffle away.

"Politics as usual," one echoed.

They couldn't have known that a completely new alliance was being forged right before their eyes—and one that would benefit them—breaking the cycle of oppression and corruption that had kept them as second-class citizens for as long as any of their people could remember.

Later, when he was asked about that fateful meeting, the taxman said, "The governor told me I didn't have to keep taking from the people to secure my future. He was going to take care of me. You know, I was always going for my own security by exploiting the system. My old cronies should have fired me. Somehow when this new governor offered me his hand and called me by name, it just deeply touched me. Everybody in his new administration is there because of him alone. Just knowing him gives a person a generous heart. That's all I can tell you."

That afternoon the taxman announced that half of the debtors under his watch were to be released from their debts upon his signature. And he also agreed to pay back the funds he'd pilfered and start a foundation for the defense of those who couldn't afford a lawyer. Furthermore, he would personally fund organizations to help with education, job training, and housing for the local community.

It was a day the town and the taxman would never forget. They called it the day love came to their town.

How New Life Changes Everything

The taxman's transformation from hard-hearted, corrupt official to generous heart is actually the story of Zacchaeus in Luke 19:1–9.

Zacchaeus, a corrupt tax collector, rose above his circumstances when he climbed a tree to get a glimpse of Jesus passing through Jericho en route to Jerusalem. They met early on the day we now mark as Palm Sunday, the day the Jewish people declared Jesus their king as he rode into the holy city (Luke 19:38). This was no ordinary day and no ordinary crowd that showed up to greet Jesus. The people exulted, shouting, "Hosanna," praises for the king promised of old to save them and rescue them as God's own. Jesus was to be their liberator from the Roman oppressors, the one who would restore them as God's chosen people. Their champion had come!

Why was Zacchaeus celebrating the end of his reign of economic terror on his fellow Jews?

He was likely to be shunned by the clamoring crowd that would have loathed every tax collector for the brutality and hardship they wrought. And Zacchaeus was not only that but a wealthy man amid the poor (v. 2). His wealth could only have come from extracting bribes and otherwise stealing from his own people, abusing his place in government to harm them financially. You can understand the people's dismay then by Jesus singling out Zacchaeus as someone he knew by name.

That is how Jesus greeted Zacchaeus. "I must stay at your house today," Jesus said (v. 5).

As far as the Jews were concerned, traitors like Zacchaeus were part of the reason they needed and welcomed a king. Tax collectors had stolen from them. Yet Jesus chose this one man and offered to meet with him at his home.

Why did Jesus single out Zacchaeus?

The Bible tells us Zacchaeus wanted to see who Jesus was (v. 3). The tax collector may have been despised by the crowd, but when he climbed up to see Jesus, his desire drew Jesus' attention. People weren't happy about Jesus' response. Some even doubted if he really was to be king. That very day, however, the crowd saw the almighty power of the love of Christ when the greedy traitor Zacchaeus suddenly became the benefactor of the poor. Making restitution moved Zacchaeus from one spiritual state to the other. Before the meeting, Zacchaeus was always looking for ways to line his pocket; after, he not only gave away half his wealthy estate, but he made restitution four times over to those he had cheated (v. 8). This act of restitution healed his heart. Once he returned his wealth, his required penalty was paid to God, and his guilt was forgiven. All this happened publicly so that all would know he was returned to good standing in the Temple courts.

Giving changes you from the inside out

The idea of grace, of unmerited pardon that Jesus granted Zacchaeus, was foreign to most Jews in Zacchaeus's day. Jewish law called for an official guilt offering in the Temple for various crimes of taking money from others (Lev. 6:1–7). Zacchaeus recognized Jesus as ruler of the Temple with his pledge of restitution above the specific penalty God and the priest demanded for the crime of extortion (Luke 19:8). This assured God's forgiveness under Old Testament law (Lev. 6:7), and helped him regain the trust of those he had harmed by his abuse. His payment did not buy his pardon, but rather was an outward sign to others of a radical change of heart.

Restitution is no longer required of New Testament believers, but we can learn a great deal by studying the principles governing godly restoration. According to *Holman Bible Dictionary*:

> Old Testament law established a principle of "punishment to fit the crime" (life for life, eye for eye, tooth for tooth, wound for

wound). Restitution was consistent with this concept of equity. The stolen property was to be returned, or "full" compensation was to be made. The guidelines for making complete restitution also included a provision for punitive damages (up to five times what had been lost), justice that moved beyond "an eye for an eye." . . . The act of making restitution to a victim was so closely identified with the atoning sacrifice made to God, that the two expressions could be seen as elements of the same command. Neither could stand alone. . . . There is no legal or ritual application of this command in the New Testament; however, the principle of restitution is clearly pictured in the story of Zacchaeus (Luke 19:1–10). Jesus implicitly validated the practice when he admonished followers to "be reconciled" to a brother before offering a gift to God (Matthew 5:23–24).[1]

As forgiven and redeemed citizens of our infinitely rich king (Phil. 3:20), we are inspired by the Holy Spirit to acts of love as evidence of our proper regard for having taken what was never ours to take—a precious human life—that which we never can repay. In Jesus' kingdom, saving faith makes us his citizens, and giving becomes our outward sign that God has healed our hearts of selfishness and sin by helping us care for others. This is especially true after abortion.

This is the final spiritual problem of abortion—we treated our children as our property when the body, blood, and tissue of an unborn child are the sacred property of God. No human can manufacture human flesh, and that means it is never ours to buy, sell, or destroy; so there is no human way to possibly atone and make restitution for our wrong.

In our new life, we recognize Christ as our sin offering to atone for the blood of the child we allowed to be killed, and Jesus is our guilt offering assuring us full pardon for all sin (Rom. 8:3–4). When Jesus comes, our king of our hearts takes us not by force, but he wins us by his love. We become a "new creation; the old has gone, the new has come!" (2 Cor. 5:17). There is no payment we can give to make good on such a taken treasure as the life of an unborn child, yet giving to others for God's cause is one practical action we can take to outwardly express our inner change of heart. According to his everlasting standard—begun in Leviticus and reiterated in the New Testament (Luke 7:47)—those grateful for pardon should be givers. Yes, God wants our money, but even more, he wants our hearts. He wants a giving heart and a lifestyle of demonstrating it—not because that is what saves us, but because giving is our joy, expressing our deep care for others, a by-product of our love.

Imagine the conversation then in Luke 19:5–9 between Jesus and Zacchaeus that day as they arrived at the splendid (ill-gotten) estate:

ZACCHAEUS [excited and filled with joy]: Please, sit here. I'm not sure how you knew my name, but it's certainly an honor to have you here in my home. The word is you are to be king, can it really be true?

JESUS [warmly]: What do you think, Zacchaeus?

ZACCHAEUS: I wasn't sure, but seeing you today, I really believe it!

JESUS: Assuming you are right, what would that mean to you?

ZACCHAEUS: Salvation for our people! This lousy job as tax collector for the Romans has cost me my family and friends. A king for Israel would mean our land would return to us, and I could quit.

JESUS: You're close. But my reign is also going to include a new constitution, not only abolishing the tax on my people, but giving citizenship to whoever opens his or her heart in complete obedience to me.

ZACCHAEUS: My Lord, I want to be part of your kingdom!

JESUS: Done. Some changes are in order as to how you've been conducting business, and this lavish lifestyle you've been living, as I think you know.

ZACCHAEUS: Gladly, Lord! What a relief to give to your people instead of always taking. I'm going to go out of my way to help the ones I've hurt.

JESUS: And that is what I always wanted.

In their actual encounter, Jesus next ratified the faith of Zacchaeus and his pledge of restitution by saying to him, "Today salvation has come to this house, because this man, too, is a son of Abraham. For the Son of Man came to seek and to save what was lost" (Luke 19:9–10).

Jesus accepted Zacchaeus's offer of restitution as evidence of his changed heart. When Jesus assured Zacchaeus's salvation, he gave hope to all lost people who have destroyed the lives of others. No one is beyond Jesus' power to save. Jesus redeems our worst mistakes to his greatest glory.

Even a hated and despised man like Zacchaeus became a blessing to others when Jesus' love changed him and created in him a giving heart.

Zacchaeus reminds me of Charles Dickens's old miser, Ebenezer Scrooge, who encountered love at Christmastime. A supernatural intervention showed Scrooge the ugly and painful future result of his past coveting and coldness of heart, awakening him to a new life of giving love, starting right away. Mirth and generosity poured forth in equal measure to his former dour spirit of doom. Just as Scrooge went and blessed everyone he had harmed, and especially Tiny Tim, Jesus' love moved Zacchaeus to give to the poor and repay those he had cheated in the past.

Truly encountering and placing our wholehearted faith in the love of Jesus Christ makes us overflow with gratitude and love, like springs of living water (John 7:38). Woe to us if we try to pervert God's holy purpose by trying to buy approval from God or people with our money or material goods (Matt. 23:23). Serving or giving to *atone* or "pay" for our sin, or to look good, or out of a sense of religious obligation is a sure recipe for spiritual frustration and can never get at the root of the problem. Welcoming the love of Jesus Christ into your life is something different altogether. You believe he paid to ransom you from a death sentence, and receive him as your Savior. As you follow, he truly becomes your Lord. Then out of your wholeness, it becomes your joy to go and give.

— **TIMELESS TRUTH**
Jesus redeems our worst mistakes to his greatest
glory when we go and give.

Giving increases your love

Some will always refuse to accept God's grace with a response of faith, just like the crowd upset that Jesus recognized Zaccheaus. Some people will determine in their hearts that God couldn't possibly forgive after abortion.

"It's too good to be true," they will say.

For them, for most of us, God's gift of grace to forgive abortion, along with every other sin, is just too much to grasp.

But each one of us who accept God's grace becomes filled to overflowing with joy like Zaccheaus, eager to give our gifts and express our love by any means we can. This was what happened to my heart when I met a girl I'll call "Larissa."

At a worship concert just months after I'd been redeemed of my abortion, volunteers from Compassion International distributed information about children living in poverty. A friend took a packet, reached across three people, and put it in my hands.

No! I thought. *I wasn't thinking of making this commitment tonight, God. I didn't agree to this.* I would never have taken a packet. Why did my friend pass this to me? Then I looked down at the photo of a nine-year-old girl from the Philippines, understanding a child had literally been put in my hands. I read her name.

As I peered into her pretty face the Holy Spirit spoke into my heart, saying, *Kim, no more throwaway children.*

God was asking me to give to a child in need, to love a child just as he had done for mine.

So that is what my husband and I did. We sponsored Larissa as the Lord taught me to love beyond myself. I could never make up for my spiritual deficiency when I had an abortion, but I could show love to a child in need by giving now out of my financial means and blessing. As my husband and I sowed into Larissa's life with letters and support, God enlarged my motherly heart with even more love than had been there before. Here was a child who needed material support, which cost us so little to give. Here was a child eager to know about Jesus, which took so little time to write in the letters we exchanged. Here was hope that I could become someone who lived beyond my own daily concerns as I prayed for her family and church half a world away. Here was the gospel come to life as God gave us a chance to care for one of his poor ones simply out of our love and listening to the heart of Jesus Christ.

Giving keeps on giving

God heals each of us as we exercise motherly or fatherly love toward a child now as a way to honor your child lost to abortion. This includes the children God has given you to parent. Remember that no child can atone for the life of a child lost to abortion. Each child is a unique creation of the almighty God and not a single one of them is like any other.

For me, this means honoring and loving both my own children, Sam and Addie, and my stepchildren, Jason and Emily, as separate and distinct individuals whose lives bear no comparison to any other. To me, each of these beautiful children represents God's graciousness toward me and my own life redeemed. The privilege of parenting includes loving each child strictly for who they are. Just as it would be unjust and unfair to them to view any child's worth in light of another child lost to abortion, it is also a tribute to all children when God expands the borders of our hearts as we give to honor the memory of a child we have in heaven.

My husband and I were blessed with a chance to meet Larissa five years later as we traveled for my work in Christian broadcasting to the Philippines with her sponsoring agency, Compassion International. Compassion works on behalf of children in poverty all around the world and in your backyard, all of whom need our love. In Manila, we saw the impact of poverty that robs children of opportunity, health, and hope. We met the city's tomb-dwellers, families with children whose homes are in a cemetery in one-room lean-tos smaller than the average

American guest closet. We also visited other urban squatter communities housing children whose parents live on less than one dollar a day. As we met the children being released from poverty in the Compassion child development centers, we saw that compared to the rest of the world, we have so much to give. A few dollars to supply nutritious meals and basic immunizations could determine whether a child will have a chance to grow and thrive within the safety of fellowship of the local church, or whether they will remain outside, abandoned to the streets.

Compassion arranged for Larissa's first-ever trip from her home island of Palawan to meet us in Manila. Since it was almost time for her birthday, we went on a shopping spree—Larissa's first trip to a modern mall. She navigated an escalator for the first time that day. And we found out what new school clothes and shoes can mean to a girl who might have been forced into the world of adult unskilled labor without them. Her joy and gratitude were as heartwarming as her sacrificial gift to me—pearls that I know came at great price to her chronically underemployed family back home.

As our visit came to an end, we asked if there was anything else she would especially like to take home.

She thought for a minute and then answered, "Yes, please. I share a bed with my younger brother, and I would like to have a blanket of my own."

Love is like that—it covers a multitude of sins and spills out of you to redeem others, who in turn pass it along.

The Giving Heart

Jesus giving grace after abortion is the point of departure for many. By our track record we may represent a ridiculous risk as ministry or leadership candidates, especially by those who are sensitive to the widespread loss of life. Millions of children have died—has God really restored our reputation in his own eyes? What about the children? Will God simply forget?

Although grace is always surprising and often runs counter to our expectations and judgments, by granting grace, God can never be unjust.

My seeing Jesus suffer on the cross made me fall to my knees and ask that he put the hurt on me. Instead of punishing, he told me to go and give his love. Worship is God's desired response to encountering his grace. As we bow, he always directs us in new paths. Some people will bow down, realize his holiness, and still refuse to believe or obey his love. The rich young ruler stood up and walked away (Mark 10:17–22). He sadly trusted something other than Jesus' heavenly promise of future treasure for doing what God requires of us in this life. And then there is Zacchaeus, who received his pardon and responded with gratitude and love—what Jesus wished for all along—by giving away his wealth, the thing that he had held most dear.

Shortly after his highly successful ministry launch, Jesus returned to his hometown and went to the synagogue to affirm God's ancient promises to his people (Luke 4:17–21). Jesus cast a vision for love as his kingly mission that day in Nazareth. The vision began with the anointing by the Holy Spirit to preach God's protective love of the poor; he proclaimed freedom for prisoners, sight for the blind, an end to oppression, all taking place in a time of favor from the Lord.

Then he made this shocking statement, "Today this scripture is fulfilled in your hearing" (Luke 4:21).

The people got it. For a brief moment, he was the hometown hero.

When Jesus reminded these people of God's grace in granting miracles to outsiders (Luke 4:25–27), the people weren't too excited about Jesus implying their oppressors, the murdering Romans, were being invited along into the new kingdom he had come to establish. Yet God in Christ forgives every sin, and exercises justice by establishing his people as protectors of the weak.

At this, the hometown crowd became enraged and ran him to the outskirts of town intending to throw him off a cliff. Grace would be a scandal to the victim of oppression or a crime apart from God's full plan in Jesus Christ. The problem was not that these people had never encountered Jesus. They just didn't like what he had to say.

The situation is no different today. We can be astounded by his love as we bow down to our King, trusting his plan, rising new and healed. Or, we can let our own ideas limit his power and influence in our lives.

One woman, Vivian, reflects, "When I regarded abortion as 'the unforgivable sin,' I was not open to the healing grace of Jesus Christ and it was just as if he had never died for me. But now that I believe he loves me and my child in heaven, I know that he would never turn away anyone who is truly sorry for their sins, and who believes in his power to forgive." Finding this faith meant that Vivian had to listen to God's voice above the opinions of others—even at times the opinions of others in the church.

Among the people who encountered Jesus in his hometown of Nazareth, "He could not do any miracles there, except lay his hands on a few sick people and heal them. And he was amazed at their lack of faith" (Mark 6:5–6).

Spiritual character repair and healing comes today as we honor God's scandalous grace by making restitution, signaling our guilty days are over. We change and begin anew, leaving the old way of life (Matt. 3:2, 8). And since we now live by the Spirit, we make every effort to keep in step with the Holy Spirit (Gal. 5:25). We freely give the good news of the gift of healing we have received that others may be healed (Matt. 10:7–8). All of this comes to us spiritually through faith (Heb. 11:6). God heals our lives, rewarding our faith with joy, hope, and peace where once our spirits were broken in despair (Isa. 61:1–3).

We need not work for the precious gifts of God. What price could we possibly pay? We simply need to know and trust God to meet his responsibilities, and we need to know and meet our own. What price will it be your joy to now repay?

The way I sought to prove my worth had always been my work. I tried to forget the pain of abortion by throwing myself into my broadcasting career. It was a faulty foundation of self-reliance that only added to how I'd forsaken the life of my unborn child. God kindly provided many material blessings for me, and I loved the work. But to believe that a career and its rewards would heal me and help me pay for my poor choice was to believe a lie. There can never be peace in placing career or anything else above a human life. I was "eat[ing] the bread of sorrow," as the Scriptures say (Psalm 127:2 NKJV), and from my labor, I learned, "Unless the LORD builds the house, its builders labor in vain" (Ps. 127:1).

Even absent career ambitions, abortion so often comes down to economics. Fear of poverty is a prime motivator for many. One woman says, "I grew up with a single mom and I wanted to break the cycle—no child of mine would grow up poor. But now I just wish I had that child with me to love and care for."

A related motivator is worry over the loss of status, which also has its roots in lifestyle and money. Another woman explained, "My boyfriend offered to marry me, but the stereotype of a shotgun wedding was mortifyingly impossible for me to picture."

In a busy airport one day not long ago, I saw all the well-dressed women and men in suits and wondered who among them was the one out of every four[2] carrying the sorrow of a lost child along with smart briefcases and expensive luggage. I thought of how I had been one of those covering my sorrow with the trappings of a suit and a briefcase and a career. *How far would I have been able to advance if I had stepped away to become a mom? And how had it damaged my own heart to have sacrificed a child as a stepping-stone to success?*

Abortion costs something, but we get it so wrong as to what exactly. For some, abortion is thought to save the financial cost of raising a child. For others, it's the choice to save one's self from emotional costs, such as a forever tether to an unsanctioned or unhappy or unpleasant union.

Whether we are rich or poor when we face abortion, most of us choose it because of what we think it will save us from, some future threat in economic terms.[3] We ignore or fail to see the cost of abortion to our soul, our selves—and to others. But God is merciful. Christ, even from the cross, is forgiving. God, in his mercy, redeems even the choice to build our house on our children's innocent blood when we now choose to believe that Christ's shed blood has forgiven us and that he will make us new. Each of us is needy and undeserving. We can only rely on rescue by the grace of God, who pursues us and offers us grace from sin and death whenever we call on him by faith. More than this, we receive our rescue completely free of charge. Giving is a tangible way to express our joy over what the Lord has done for us.

Jesus said, "He who hears My word and believes in Him who sent Me has everlasting life, and shall not come into judgment, but has passed from death into life" (John 5:24 NKJV). No further punishment is required than the penalty Christ paid when he died for us on the cross.

His words still pierce my heart just as they do in every encounter with God's love. He says, *Believe. Forgive. Love. Live.* He has cradled our hearts in order to help us pick up our lives again and walk away from the selfishness of sin just like the lame man healed at the pool. I hope you can join me in saying he has satisfied our thirsty souls and pointed the way to worship him in spirit and in truth, making us like the woman at the well—eager to go and tell. He defeated death, making us clean, mercifully praying on our behalf. And Jesus has forever lifted us up from a life lived apart from his almighty love. He has given us a bridge of heavenly hope by which we gain a future filled with peace.

Jesus has paid the penalty for abortion and holds our child in heaven. Our eternal life with him and with them is now and forever secure.

What will you be inspired to give him in return?

The Cradled Heart

God is always writing our life stories through circumstances we can seldom imagine.

Several years ago my sister learned she was ill with kidney disease as a result of a condition that was not genetic, not inherited. But she needed a kidney transplant and without one her chances of survival would diminish—and soon. I traveled to her hometown to see if I might help. I went through a battery of medical tests and learned I was a donor match. With very little hesitation, I agreed that I would give a kidney if it meant that she might be restored to full health. I love my sister, and after so many years of feeling so very helpless to ease her long struggle, I was ready and willing to come to her aid.

But then her doctor said donating a kidney wasn't necessary just yet. Her illness was not systemic, so she was able to survive for a number of years with very limited kidney function. She moved cross-country, and was holding steady. We each continued on with our lives.

However, she eventually reached an end stage with her disease and had to begin dialysis. I was tested again and things were still favorable for me to give her one of my kidneys, so we made the decision to go ahead with a transplant.

Though Cyb is my older sister, she is petite compared to me. She always complained when we shared clothes as teenagers that whatever I wore of hers was always returned "stretched out." The kidney I gave her was no different. Following the procedure, her surgeon remarked that all had gone well, but my kidney was so robust that when it was first placed in my sister's abdomen, it popped right back out!

The good news was, even though that big old kidney stretched her out, her function was normal within forty-eight hours without any signs of rejection. So my kidney became her kidney in March of 2009 and she has recovered completely. So have I. Some of my loved ones were worried about the surgical risk to me, but God gave me courage, and I can honestly say I approached the day without fear. You can imagine my joy knowing she has resumed her life and is now prospering in her career, marriage, and her role today as a wife and mother, and grandmother of two.

Do you see how God has completely rewritten my story? He changed me from one who acted in a cowardly, selfish fashion to take a life, and made me into one willing to lay down my life out of love for another. What a gift—to me! God arranged our circumstances and used me to share a life-saving gift with someone I love so much.

That same gift is yours. As you follow Jesus, you will see his opportunities for selfless giving. You'll find your cradled, healed heart is whole—in order for you to share with others as Christ did, does, and will always do.

Jesus' encounters show us how to give to those impoverished in mind, body, and spirit, just as we were after abortion. I've learned that as you draw near to him in prayer, he will draw near to you (James 4:8). At times this may mean that you are called out of your comfort zone to love and care for someone very unlike yourself—he will give you a heart to cradle as your very own. New roles in your church and new relationships with friends in faith will come your way. As you continue on in your journey through this life with Christ, remember those affected by abortion like you. Give to the cause of America's unborn children in need of our care.

John Ensor is an ordained minister who left his pastorate to work in the pregnancy help movement first in Boston, then in Miami, and now throughout the world through Heartbeat International. He has helped me understand that abortion is always a personal, local issue in communities. "Children are not just perishing in the capitol in Washington, D.C." he says. "They are losing their lives in our neighborhoods."[4]

He means to make abortion an issue of your heart, and not just your politics. Move beyond abortion rhetoric by giving to a local pregnancy care center. This is a lovely act of restitution whether through your time, your talents, or your wealth. Ensor calls this work, "Saving innocent lives one woman at a time."[5]

Think about providing foster care or adoption for children in need. Your home and your heart are needed right now today regardless of what has happened in your past.

Better yet, devote your life to thinking upon the cross of Jesus Christ. It was there that I found the love of God that has healed my heart. Before I felt this amazing love and sacrifice, I had a daily ritual of showing up in prayer and saying, "Use me, Lord."

That's a good place to start your life of faith with him. But before the Lord honors that prayer, he captures our heart with his love. After I grasped all that Jesus has done for me, I was also given a new heart's cry. I tell him now, "I'm yours." This is the attitude Jesus inspires as he lifts our heads to sing his love. Our champion takes only willing volunteers, and his Holy Spirit makes us so. Psalm 110:3 (NKJV) says:

> Your people shall be volunteers
> In the day of Your power;
> In the beauties of holiness, from the womb of the morning,
> You have the dew of Your youth.

This is he: our Lord and Savior, Jesus Christ, ever young, ever faithful, ever tender, ever true.

Live to love God, and love others as yourself, for "love covers over a multitude of sins" (1 Peter 4:8). Don't give up until you see God's joy reflected in relationships centered upon the love of Jesus Christ. He loves you. You are his and you are free to love and grow.

Remember, God writes the best endings. Think of all the ways he has given you opportunities to be someone new, so that "just as Christ was raised from the dead through the glory of the Father, we too may live a new life" (Rom. 6:4).

He has always been there to cradle your heart. And he remains there to grant you his peace.

—— *Reflect* ————————————————————————

Read for yourself the account of Zacchaeus in Luke 19, a portrait of the life-changing love of Christ. Now think upon these passages:

- "I will not forget you! See, I have engraved you on the palms of my hands" (Isa. 49:15–16).
- "Give your bodies to God because of all he has done for you. . . . Then you will learn to know God's will for you, which is good and pleasing and perfect" (Rom. 12:1–2 NLT).
- "Therefore, if you are offering your gift at the altar and there remember that your brother has something against you, leave your gift there in front of the altar. First go and be reconciled to your brother; then come and offer your gift" (Matt. 5:23–24).
- "Therefore, since we have been justified through faith, we have peace with God through our Lord Jesus Christ, through whom we have gained access by faith into this grace in which we now stand. And we rejoice in the hope of the glory of God. Not only so, but we also rejoice in our sufferings, because we know that suffering produces perseverance; perseverance, character; and character, hope. And hope does not disappoint us, because God has poured out his love into our hearts by the Holy Spirit, whom he has given us" (Rom. 5:1–5).
- "Arise, shine, for your light has come, and the glory of the LORD rises upon you" (Isa. 60:1).
- "They will be called oaks of righteousness, a planting of the LORD

for the display of his splendor. They will rebuild the ancient ruins and restore the places long devastated . . . for generations" (Isa. 61:3–4).

- "I am still confident of this: I will see the goodness of the LORD in the land of the living. Wait for the LORD; be strong and take heart and wait for the LORD" (Ps. 27:13–14).
- "For I am convinced that neither death nor life, neither angels nor demons, neither the present nor the future, nor any powers, neither height nor depth, nor anything else in all creation, will be able to separate us from the love of God that is in Christ Jesus our Lord" (Rom. 8:38–39).

—— *Request* ————————————————————————

Lord, I praise you for mercifully giving me new birth into a living hope through the resurrection of Jesus from the dead. Thank you for an inheritance that can never spoil or fade. Thank you for accepting my gifts offered in loving memory and as restitution toward harm done to children in the past. May I never forget to honor your little ones. In faith, I await what you have kept in heaven for me. Thank you for faith that shields me by your power until the coming day when you will bring everything under your rule. This is my prayer of your Word in 1 Peter 1:3–5. I ask these things in Jesus' name. Amen.

—— *Respond* ————————————————————————

- Foster new life by supporting a pregnancy help center as a volunteer or donor.
- Sponsor a child through Compassion International, World Vision, or another world mission. As you come to know a child personally through corresponding, you may begin to see the world as both bigger and smaller than you have viewed it in the past. Seeing the child's picture, praying for his or her faith and well-being, caring beyond yourself will help you grow in Christ. Ask God to provide funds, or to re-order your spending priorities, so that you may become more generous to the poor. Sponsorship costs can be as

low as $1.25 a day (Americans generally spend three times that amount each year on our pets—consider matching at least a portion of the expense of caring for your beloved pet to begin caring for a child in need.)

- Take an hour a week to read to children at a local school or library. Nurture children in the church nursery or other setting where you can give hands-on care.
- Donate blood or other life-giving gifts (even your hair could mean joy for a child who is seriously ill—see Locks of Love online at www.locksoflove.org).
- Beautify your worship center with altar flowers in memory of your child in heaven. This can be especially meaningful as a holiday remembrance when combined with memorials for other family members who are being honored.
- Listen to or sing these hymns and songs of praise for God's tender mercy and goodness: "How Great Is Your Faithfulness" by Jonas Myrin and Matt Redman (an anthem to the realm of our hearts where God's faithful love reigns supreme); "Shine" by the Newsboys to energize and motivate you to love more like God; "You Raise Me Up," by Rolf Lovland and Brendan Graham and performed by Selah, which can inspire faith that God can totally change us and make us better than we ever dreamed; and "Thank You," written by Timothy Burgess and sung by The Katinas, which acknowledges the great debt we owe Jesus, the gracious source of strength for every grateful heart.

Acknowledgments

My deepest thanks and appreciation go to many:

Everyone at Kregel Publications, especially Dennis Hillman, Steve Barclift, and Cat Hoort, for encouraging all who need to know and encounter the transforming power and everlasting promises we may lay hold of through knowledge of God's Word.

My literary agent, Les Stobbe, whose vision and direction helped shape this work to more fully reflect the broad range of lives changed by encountering God's love.

Jeanette Thomason, who polished my words, helping God's love shine. Fellow writer and friend in faith, Susie Larson, who encouraged in countless ways; and Julie Smith and Gwen Ellis who gave good guidance early on. Ruth Graham and Friends ministry partners: Ruth Graham, Tex and Sandy Reardon, Don Miles, Linda Mintle, Tal Prince, Huntley Brown, Aleta Nichols, Jacquie Skog, Steve Wiese, Cheryl Torain, Jason Catron, Jim and Mary Whitmer, and Dr. Jimmy Ray Lee, thank you for love and constant edification.

The staff and volunteers at New Life Family Services in Richfield, Minnesota, who helped me live out the healing love of Christ with my child in heaven; and to all serving in postabortion ministry, especially through the pregnancy help movement. Without you, my message has little meaning. You are the hands and feet of Jesus Christ to families in need. Special thanks to the Rev. John Ensor for encouragement and support along the way.

The men and women who have shared their stories with me. All names have been changed in the profile stories, and composite quotes reflect experiences shared in common. Also thanks to the experts who have helped me gain spiritual insight and wisdom. Without your stories and witness to God's healing truth, this book would not be possible.

My prayer partners, who believed and interceded when my energy and confidence flagged, and whose faith has helped me see. To my sample readers Rafael Zarate, Dorothy Fleming, Jackie Arnold, Tina Schneider, Kim Hardy, and Ruth Plunkett. Your time and attention mean the world to me.

My family—my husband, Bruce, whose love and support are a blessing beyond measure; to my children, Sam and Addie, who have taught me what it means to love with a mother's heart, you are my life redeemed; and to my stepchildren, Jason and Emily, who have enlarged this mother's heart. To my siblings, Cynthia, Robert, Grady, and Matthew, to whom I belong as both sister and friend. May each of you always know my love for you, and the love of Jesus Christ.

Most of all, thanks to my Lord and Savior, Jesus Christ, who is my role model, teaching me to live life full of God's grace and truth.

Helpful Resources

M ore organizations and agencies are stepping up to help women and men after abortion. While this contains some of the most helpful, it's not comprehensive, and inclusion here does not imply an affiliation or endorsement by the author. This list is simply a good place to start. Exercise your own discretion as you seek help, and ask in your church and public service community for additional local, regional, and international organizations that offer resources and care.

Help After Abortion

All calls to these hotlines offer free and confidential assistance and referrals.

Abortion Recovery InterNational's CARE Directory & CARE Line is an international network of Abortion Recovery Centers and Programs that provide healing opportunities to those hurting after abortion at 1-866-4-My-Recovery (469-7326) and online at www.abortionrecovery.org.

National Helpline for Abortion Recovery has trained phone and mail consultants who help locate the abortion recovery program nearest you. Call 1-866-482-LIFE or visit them online at www.nationalhelpline.org. Calls are answered 24/7.

Word of Hope offers comfort to women hurting from a past abortion. Call 1-888-217-8679 or visit them online at www.word-of-hope.org.

Help with Pregnancy-Related Decisions

Option Line connects you to help with pregnancy decisions as well as referrals for care after abortion. Calls are answered 24/7 at 1-800-712-HELP (4357). Or for chat and email help, visit www.optionline.org or www.heartbeatinternational.org.

Pregnancy Decision Line connects you to help with pregnancy decisions and referrals for care after abortion. Call 1-800-395-HELP (4357), or for chat and email help visit www.pregnancydecisionline.org.

Hotlines for Help with Abortion-Related Crisis Issues

Domestic violence requires immediate help for threats or violent actions. Call 911. For long-term care, consider Life Skills International training, available online at www.lifeskillsintl.org.

Suicide intervention offers immediate help for thoughts, plans, or actions toward suicide or serious self-harm. Call 911 or 1-800-273-TALK (8255).

Counseling Resources

Abortion Recovery InterNational (ARIN) is a Christian affiliate association of peer counselors, licensed professionals, and pastoral leaders who are dedicated to restoring lives and relationships after abortion; find training and resources online at www.arininc.org.

American Association of Christian Counselors offers The Christian Care Network (CCN), a national referral network of state licensed, certified, and/or properly credentialed Christian counselors offering care that is distinctively Christian and clinically excellent; find a counselor at www.aacc.net.

PACE Post Abortion Peer Counseling and Education is an outreach of Care Net pregnancy centers, www.care-net.org.

Project Rachel is a network of specially trained caregivers in Catholic churches through The National Office of Post Abortion Reconciliation and Healing. Call 1-800-5WE-CARE, or visit them online at www.hopeafterabortion.com.

Online Bible Studies, Help, and Support

Free Me to Live: Recovery Course is an interactive, online study to overcome abortion at www.freemetolive.com. Last Harvest Ministries also provides a variety of resources at www.freemetolive.com.

Safe Haven Ministries is an online message board at www.safehavenministries.com.

For Men

Fatherhood Forever offers abortion recovery for men; visit them online at www.fatherhoodforever.org.

Life Issues Institute resources for men and women include email support, articles, books, and brochures online at www.lifeissues.org.

Men and Abortion offers support and helpful research of the challenges men face after abortion; visit them online at www.menandabortion.info.

Missing Arrows, A Bible Study About Lost Fatherhood by Warren Williams is available digitally for free download online at www.lifeissues.org/men/missingarrows.pdf.

Ministry for and by African Americans

Everlasting Light Ministries offers help with recovery after abortion, marriage enrichment, and divorce prevention at www.everlastinglightministries.org.

LEARN, Life Education and Resource Network is a national network raising awareness and equipping the African American church for the sanctity of life, study of eugenics, www.blackgenocide.org.

The National Black Prolife Coalition is working to end abortion by restoring a culture of life and family in the black community; www.blackprolifecoalition.org.

The Radiance Foundation promotes adoption and family values in the African American community; www.radiancefoundation.org.

Healing Retreats

Rachel's Vineyard offers weekend retreats for women, men, and couples in a confidential and caring environment; 1-877-HOPE-4-ME (467-3463), or online at www.rachelsvineyard.org.

Research and Awareness

American Victims of Abortion is a broad-based public awareness campaign with resources online at www.nrlc.org/outreach/AVA.html.

The Eliot Institute presents online research, education, and advocacy for those hurt by abortion at www.afterabortion.org.

Eternal Perspectives Ministries from Randy Alcorn has an extensive resource link online at www.epm.org/resources/2010/Apr/14/prolife-resource-list/.

Life Redeemed is a radio and podcast feature presenting stories of healing in Christ after abortion and help with expert commentary. Visit the archived broadcasts online at www.liferedeemed.org.

The National Pro-Life Religious Council presents an annual Memorial Service for the Pre-born and their Mothers and Fathers in Washington, D.C., every January. Council members represent Anglicans, CEC, Conservative Congregational, United Methodists, Missouri Synod Lutherans, Roman Catholic, Presbyterians, and United Church of Christ clergy and ministers. Information and resources online at www.nprcouncil.org.

Operation Outcry is a global justice ministry working to end the pain of abortion, offering resources online at www.operationoutcry.org.

Silent No More Awareness is a grassroots campaign that breaks the silence of abortion by offering outreach and support online at www.silentnomoreawareness.org.

Books on Heaven

Hayford, Jack. *I'll Hold You in Heaven: Healing and Hope for the Parent Who Has Lost a Child Through Miscarriage, Stillbirth, Abortion, or Early Infant Death.* Ventura, CA: Regal, 1990.

MacArthur, John. *Safe in the Arms of God: Truth from Heaven About the Death of a Child.* Nashville: Thomas Nelson, 2003.

Alcorn, Randy. *Heaven.* Wheaton, Illinois: Tyndale, 2004.

Child Sponsorship Organizations

Compassion International is dedicated to "releasing children from poverty in Jesus' name," and can be found online at www.compassion.com.

World Vision is focused on "building a better world for children," and can be found online at www.worldvision.org.

— *Appendix B* ————————————————————

Study and Discussion Questions

A bortion is an intensely personal topic, so I'm glad Jesus loves us enough to know and care what is in our hearts. He already knows us even better than we can know ourselves, and is always available to listen, care, and help. Just as he provided wine for a wedding feast, healed the ailing child, rebuked the self-righteous, and comforted those grieving the death of a loved one, Jesus is ever-ready to give us just what we need. And he always brings together people with the most varied personal experiences to fulfill a greater purpose. That's why, as you draw closer to Christ in Bible study, it can be so meaningful to add healthy friendships. In fact, studying and praying together are essential activities for animating and activating your faith.

So, as you develop your relationship with God through the hope in Jesus Christ after abortion, this guide will help you find a starting place of fellowship too. To get the most from this book for a group study, have everyone read the chapter and complete the exercises found there, then come together to discuss these questions. Think of this as an exercise in how to grow together as friends in faith—friends who will listen in love and pray you through whatever issues press upon you. As you study together, keep in mind:

Confidentiality is mandatory. Privacy and protection of one another's vulnerability go hand-in-hand when people share their lives for the purposes of healing the pain of the past.

Bible study is not a substitute for therapy or psychological counseling. If depression or other issues require medical care, be responsible in seeking and following medical advice.

Patience is required for lasting change. Once you break the silence that may have lingered after your abortion experience, you may be eager to be free of difficult memories or personality flaws. Be sure to move at the speed of faith and not run ahead of God. Every person has specific, unique needs. Try to listen as much as you lean.

It's important to continue through the process until the study is complete. Set aside a particular time and place to meet each week and honor the commitment to one another.

Chapter 1: An Examination

1. Write down your abortion story as a way of examining it outside yourself, perhaps for the first time.
2. Jesus says we can move on from the past. Do you think abortion has limited your spiritual growth?
3. How does weak faith get built up? Can you think of other encounters between Jesus and people with weak faith? What do you learn from them?
4. As you consider the lame man at the pool, do you think there was something more than the story tells us as to how the man was healed?
5. Do you agree that the man at the pool had a problem with blaming others? Explain.

Chapter 2: An Invitation

1. Jesus says we can look to him to love us through and through. What are some of the things that make us feel unlovable after abortion?
2. Do you agree that there's a connection between misplaced faith and misplaced affections in our relationships with others?

3. How might the proper worship of God help us love others and ourselves properly?
4. Do you think the real housewife of Samaria continued to live with a man who was not her husband? Why or why not?
5. Why are our lifestyle decisions important to God?

Chapter 3: An Open Conversation

1. Have you begun to reflect on your abortion experience in writing? If not, what might help you take that step?
2. Have your views been changed by anything you've read here so far?
3. What are your thoughts about the cultural claims of abortion as "family planning"? How do you feel about the idea that the devil is a real and hateful enemy out to destroy?
4. Jesus says the devil is the father of lies. Have you recognized a lie concerning abortion?

Chapter 4: A Demonstration

1. People who have participated in abortion may not have chosen it. How might this be so?
2. Have you ever sensed what Jesus might mean in Matthew 5:8, "the pure in heart . . . will see God"?
3. How do you define holiness?
4. How you do respond to the idea of having to clean up your life before going to God?

Chapter 5: A Realization

1. Have you ever spent time in conversation with God about your most private thoughts? If so, what was the result? If not, why not?
2. Has being in church ever made you feel worse about abortion rather than better? Explain.
3. Where are you at in your relationship with Jesus? Do you feel you are growing in your love for him day by day?

4. What are some of the ways we can nurture our faith in Jesus after abortion?

Chapter 6: A Restoration

1. Have you been persuaded that abortion takes the life of a distinct, unique person?
2. As you encountered this point of view in chapter 6, was this new information? What had you previously believed?
3. Is it difficult for you to understand or trust what God says about himself? Explain.
4. What would it take for you to forgive everyone related to abortion in your past?

Chapter 7: A Jubilation

1. Do you have a mental image of heaven? What is the source of your perception of heaven?
2. Do you have a mental image of hell? What is the source of that perception?
3. Can you know with certainty where you will spend eternity? How?
4. How do you respond to the idea that unborn children and infants go straight to heaven? Does this conflict with your church's teaching? If so, would you be willing to have a conversation with your pastor to learn more in light of Scripture?

Chapter 8: A Consolation

1. How and when do you pray to Jesus about your loved ones? Has it been part of your practice to include loved ones who have died when you pray to Jesus about those you love?
2. The Bible strictly prohibits us trying to communicate directly with deceased loved ones. What is your understanding of God's wise provision for our spiritual health in this restriction?
3. Are you able to recall the details of the day of any abortion in your past?
4. How might prayer to Jesus about that day make a difference in your life today?

Chapter 9: A Dedication

1. How do you know if you are called to serve God?
2. What are some of the ways you may have heard and answered such a call?
3. What can disqualify us for service?
4. How can we return to service if we have disowned our faith, whether directly or by our actions?

Chapter 10: A Celebration

1. Restitution is distinct from salvation. What is the difference?
2. Describe the difference between repentance and restitution.
3. Describe the difference between reconciliation with God after sin and restitution to people we may have harmed.
4. Will God accept our gifts as payment for wrongdoing? In the Old Testament people had to pay to exercise justice—how do we exercise Christian justice today? Why does God encourage a lifestyle of giving?

Notes

Introduction: At the Heart of Things

1. Guttmacher Institute, "An Overview of Abortion in the United States," news release, accessed March 22, 2011, www.guttmacher .org/media/presskits/2005/06/28/abortionoverview.html.

2. Guttmacher Institute, "An Overview of Abortion in the United States," August 2011, slide and lecture presentation, slide 27: "Most Women Obtaining Abortions Report a Religious Affiliation," http:// www.guttmacher.org/presentations/ab_slides.html. Protestants account for 37%; Roman Catholics, 28%; other religious affiliations, 7%; those with no religious affiliation, 7%.

Chapter 1: An Examination

1. "The Blind in Law and Literature," *Jewish Encyclopedia* Online, Kopelman Foundation, accessed March 1, 2012, www.jewishencyclopedia .com/view.jsp?artid=1139&letter=B#ixzz0iN05tvsL.

2. Guttmacher Institute, "Facts on Induced Abortion in the United States," In Brief: Fact Sheet, August 2011, www.guttmacher.org /pubs/fb_induced_abortion.html.

3. Infertility is one of several problems that may occur after abortion. See Priscilla Coleman, "A Tidal Wave of Published Data: More Than 30 Studies in Last Five Years Show Negative Impact of Abortion on Women," Physicians for Life, November 2010, www.physiciansfor life.org/content/view/75/50/.

4. Guttmacher Institute, "Facts on Induced Abortion in the United States."

5. Eliot Institute, "Teen Abortion Risks," Fact Sheet, January 2008, http://theunchoice.com/pdf/OnePageFactSheets/TeensSheet1.pdf.

6. Rick Warren, *Life's Healing Choices*, DVD (Lake Forest, CA: Saddleback Church, 2009).

Chapter 2: An Invitation

1. Yehoshua M. Grintz, "Mount Gerizim," *Encyclopedia Judaica*, 2008, Jewish Virtual Library, The American-Israeli Co-operative Enterprise, 2010, www.jewishvirtuallibrary.org/jsource/judaica/ejud_0002_00 07_0_07198.html.

2. Guttmacher Institute, "An Overview of Abortion in the United States," August 2011, slide and lecture presentation, slide 27: "Most Women Obtaining Abortions Report a Religious Affiliation," http://www.guttmacher.org/presentations/ab_slides.html. (This presentation was originally created in collaboration with Physicians for Reproductive Choice and Health in 2003, and has been periodically updated to reflect the most current data available. This version was updated by Rachel Jones, Rebecca Wind, and Heather Boonstra of the Guttmacher Institute in 2011.)

3. Joni Erickson Tada, *Joni and Friends* radio broadcast, Joni and Friends ministry, date unknown.

4. Kathryn Kost and Stanley Henshaw, *U.S. Teenage Pregnancies, Births and Abortions, 2008: National Trends by Age, Race and Ethnicity*, Guttmacher Institute, February 2012, http://www.guttmacher.org /pubs/USTPtrends08.pdf. According to table 2.1 (p. 7), there were 192,090 abortions among women aged 15 to 19 in 2008, which means the 2008 teenage abortion rate was 17.8 abortions per 1,000 women.

5. Carole C. Carlson, *Corrie Ten Boom: Her Life, Her Faith: A Biography* (New York: Jove Books, 1984), 95.

Chapter 3: An Open Conversation

1. Shaila Dewan, "To Court Blacks, Foes of Abortion Make Racial Case," *New York Times*, February 26, 2010, http://www.nytimes .com/2010/02/27/us/27race.html.

2. Reverend Clenard H. Childress, radio interview by Kim Jeffries (Ketola), *Life Redeemed*, KTIS-FM, November 2004.

3. It's also possible Adam added the restriction; according to Genesis 2:21, when God conveyed the command to Adam, Eve had not yet been created. The apostle Paul interpreted God's pattern for marital interactions in Ephesians 5:22–33: A man is to listen to God and

protectively love his wife by conveying God's caring instructions to her; a woman is to respect what God says through listening to and trusting the man to convey the things of God to her and to their children. God never calls man or woman to submit to, lead, or follow one another apart from his guidance and direction.

4. Gary Thomas, radio interview by Kim Jeffries (Ketola), *Life Redeemed*, KTIS-FM, week of July 18, 2005.

5. Abortion practice in the Bible bears no resemblance and little relevance to a discussion of the practice of elective abortion in America today. A priestly procedure is described for enforcing marital purity and justice as the priest invited God's discernment into paternity suits (Num. 5:11–31). The priest submitted the life of the child into God's hands and then administered a ritual bitter drink that might bring the pregnancy to an end in order to protect a married man from being compelled to support a child he did not father.

6. For exposition on Psalm 106, see John Ensor, *Answering the Call: Saving Innocent Lives One Woman at a Time* (Colorado Springs: Focus on the Family, 2003).

7. The history alluded to here is recorded in 2 Kings 16:3 and 17:17–24, which recount the events leading to ongoing strife between Samaritans and Jews—strife that Jesus repeatedly sought to reconcile in the Gospels.

8. A God-commanded death penalty would not be "murder" even though it meant a violent death, since the guilty person's blood was used by God to avenge the innocent blood they took (Gen. 9:5–6).

9. John C. Fletcher and Mark I. Evans, "Maternal Bonding in Early Fetal Ultrasound Examinations," *At the Center*, www.atcmag.com/v1n1/article8.asp; originally published in the *New England Journal of Medicine* 308, no. 7 (February 17, 1983): 392–93.

10. Some religious leaders teach that abortion is acceptable to God because Genesis 2:7 says God "breathed life" into Adam, and thus a child is not alive, but just "potential life" until he or she draws a breath. "Breathing life" was a singular act that God used to animate life in all humankind. Notably, the same verse used by those religious leaders says that Adam was fashioned by God from dirt, but

God didn't replicate that use of dust to make any other full human being, not even Eve, the first offspring of Adam, who came from human tissue (his rib bone). Others teach that women have been authorized with complete moral agency from God to make the decision, so they need only answer to themselves. Both of these ideas disagree with scriptural affirmations that life begins when God creates us as eternal beings for his good purpose before conception in our mothers' wombs (Ps. 139:13–16; Isa. 46:3–4; Jer. 1:4–5). God has not revoked the command to defend the defenseless rather than shedding innocent blood; even if women have been abandoned by men, God calls others to defend her and the child (Ps. 82).

11. Edward Hinson and Edward Dobson, eds., "Fellowship Restored," *Knowing Jesus Study Bible* (Grand Rapids: Zondervan, 1999), 7.

Chapter 4: A Demonstration

1. Centers for Disease Control and Prevention, "Depression Among Women of Reproductive Age and Postpartum Depression," Division of Reproductive Health, National Center for Chronic Disease Prevention and Health Promotion, last updated December 1, 2010, http://www.cdc.gov/reproductivehealth/Depression/index.htm.

2. "Evidence did not support the claim that observed associations between abortion and mental health problems are caused by abortion per se as opposed to other preexisting and co-occurring risk factors." Brenda Major, Mark Appelbaum, Linda Beckman, et al., "Abortion and Mental Health: Evaluating the Evidence," *American Psychologist* 64, no. 9 (December 2009): 863, doi:10.1037/a0017497.

3. "As secret acts of sin, so secret acts of faith, are known to the Lord Jesus. The woman told all the truth." Matthew Henry, "The Healing of the Bloody Issue" (Mark 5:21–34), *Commentary on the Whole Bible*, vol. 5, http://www.ccel.org/ccel/henry/mhc5.Mark.vi.html.

4. Jeani Chang, Cynthia J. Berg, Linda E. Saltzman, and Joy Herndon, "Homicide: A Leading Cause of Injury Deaths Among Pregnant and Postpartum Women in the United States, 1991–1999," *American Journal of Public Health* 95, no. 3 (March 2005): 471–477, doi:10.2105/AJPH.2003.029868.

5. These practical measures were not meant to stigmatize individuals, but rather to protect "the crowd" and pursue community health (Num. 5:1–3). Along with quarantines and physical cleansing, spiritual cleansing was accomplished through sacrificial offerings. Spiritual cleansing marked out progress toward the beneficial state of being clean and thus fit to be holy, or "set apart." The ultimate purpose of attaining to holiness, the purest and most desired physical and spiritual state, was to worship. God still calls us to be holy, pursuing a perfectly pure reflection of the spotless integrity of his pure character (1 Peter 1:15–16), for "without holiness no one will see the Lord" (Heb. 12:14).

Chapter 5: A Realization

1. Kenneth Barker, ed., *Zondervan NIV Study Bible (Fully Revised)*, notes on Luke 23:34 (Grand Rapids: Zondervan, 2002).
2. Theresa Burke, radio interview by Kim Jeffries (Ketola), "Joyce's Story," *Life Redeemed*, KTIS-FM, November 2004.
3. Theresa Burke and David Reardon, *Forbidden Grief: The Unspoken Pain of Abortion* (Springfield, IL: Acorn, 2002), 167–198.
4. Philip Ney, *Deeply Damaged* (Victoria, Canada: Pioneer Publishing, 1997), 62.
5. Barker, *Zondervan NIV Study Bible*, notes on Mark 15:37.

Chapter 6: A Restoration

1. Susan Donaldson James, "Down Syndrome Births Are Down in the U.S.," ABC News, November 2, 2009, http://abcnews.go.com/Health /w_ParentingResource/down-syndrome-births-drop-us-women -abort/story?id=8960803.
2. Stephen Merritt in *Streams in the Desert*, by L. B. Cowman, updated by Jim Reimann (Grand Rapids: Zondervan, 1997), 135.
3. Randy Alcorn, *Why Pro-Life?* (Sisters, OR: Multnomah, 2004), 64.
4. Edward Goodrick and John Kohlenberger, eds. *The Strongest NIV Exhaustive Concordance*, s.v. "kilya" and s.v. "golem."
5. C. S. Lewis, *Joyful Christian: 127 Readings* (New York: Touchstone, 1996), 51.

6. Stuart Campbell, professor at Create Health Clinic in London, said, "We see the earliest movements at eight weeks. By twelve weeks or so, they are seen yawning and performing individual finger movements that are often more complex than you'll see in a newborn. It may be due to the effects of gravity after birth." *In the Womb*, "3-D and 4-D scans reveal fetal development," National Geographic Channel TV broadcast, 2005 (introductory video posted online, http://video .nationalgeographic.com/video/national-geographic-channel/all -videos/av-1539-2339/ngc-in-the-womb/ (accessed March 2, 2012).

7. *First View*, "3D and 4D Elective Ultrasound Services," http://www .firstviewultrasound.com/pricing.html; *Womb with a View*, "The Ultimate 3D/4D Ultrasound Experience," http://www.wombwithaview .com/.

8. Julie Rawe, "Sonograms R Us," *Time*, March 27, 2005, www.time .com/time/magazine/article/0,9171,1042452,00.html.

9. *NOVA*, "Life's Greatest Miracle," PBS, aired November 20, 2001, www.pbs.org/wgbh/nova/miracle/.

10. Alexi A. Wright and Ingrid T. Katz, "*Roe* Versus Reality—Abortion and Women's Health," *New England Journal of Medicine* 355 (July 6, 2006):1–9, http://www.nejm.org/doi/full/10.1056/NEJMp068083. "Each year, 1.3 million women in the United States undergo an abortion" making for a daily average of 3,561.6.

Chapter 7: A Jubilation

1. John MacArthur, *Safe in the Arms of God* (Nashville: Thomas Nelson, 2003), 6.

2. Ibid., 12–13.

3. Miriam-Webster, s.v. "indignant," accessed March 2, 2012, http:// www.merriam-webster.com/dictionary/indignant.

4. David E. Garland, *NIV Application Commentary on Mark* (Grand Rapids: Zondervan, 1996), 385.

5. MacArthur, *Safe in the Arms of God*, 33.

6. Ibid., 35.

7. Ibid., 40.

8. Ibid., 41.

Chapter 8: A Consolation

1. Oswald Chambers, "Have I Seen Him?" (April 9), *My Utmost for His Highest* (Uhrichsville, OH: Barbour, 1963).

2. Teri Reisser, radio interview by Kim Jeffries (Ketola), "Bev's Story," *Life Redeemed*, KTIS-FM, November 2004.

3. See Jeanette Vought, *Post-Abortion Trauma: 9 Steps to Recovery* (Grand Rapids: Zondervan, 1991).

4. I am grateful to Peggy Hartshorn of Heartbeat International for insight into the workings of grief and guilt in the emotional processing women experience after abortion.

5. Teri Reisser with Paul Reisser, *A Solitary Sorrow: Finding Healing and Wholeness After Abortion* (Colorado Springs: Waterbrook, 1996), 135–36.

6. Teri Reisser, radio interview by Kim Jeffries (Ketola), "Ann's Story," *Life Redeemed*, KTIS-FM, November 2004.

7. New Life Family Services, Richfield, MN, "Conquerors" curriculum (www.nlfs.org).

8. Teri Reisser interview, "Ann's Story."

9. Matthew Henry, "Not to Sorrow Unduly . . ." (1 Thessalonians 4), *Concise Commentary of the Bible*, www.biblegateway.com/resources /commentaries/Matthew-Henry/1Thess/Not-Sorrow-Unduly-Death -Godly.

Chapter 9: A Dedication

1. Sifting as wheat is what God allowed Satan to inflict on Job. Satan maligned both God and Job's faith by claiming Job didn't love God, but only the benefits God gives. If God removed his hand of blessing, Satan wagered Job would renounce God. If Satan won the bet, Job would belong to Satan. God assented to the test of Job. Things got so rough that Job's wife suggested he should curse God and die as she was suffering in Job's battle for faith—losing her children and wealth right along with all of Job's losses. But Job proved Satan's premise was wrong when he proclaimed, "The LORD gave and the LORD has taken away; may the name of the LORD be praised" (Job 1:21). God's praiseworthiness does not depend on how he treats us.

He is always good, just, and loving. You see this as God spent much time with Job, who tried to reason out all his suffering and make sense of God's ways. In the end, Job agreed with God's good wisdom and plan, and God alone has the right to run the world, and each individual life, however God sees fit. In a great twist ending, God also settled Satan's argument. When it became certain Job would worship God whether blessed or not, God went right ahead and blessed him. Job 42:10 says, "After Job had prayed for his friends the Lord made him prosperous again and gave him twice as much as he had before." This pattern of blessing after testing reveals an essential part of God's character, his trustworthy goodness and love for us, his children.

2. Peter Roff, "House Votes to Defund Planned Parenthood Over Abortion," *U.S. News and World Report* (blog), February 18, 2011, www.usnews.com/opinion/blogs/peter-roff/2011/02/18/house-votes-to-defund-planned-paerenthood-over-abortion [sic] (accessed February 23, 2011).

3. Oswald Chambers, "The Commission of the Call" (September 30), *My Utmost for His Highest* (Uhrichsville, OH: Barbour, 1963).

Chapter 10: A Celebration

1. Ken Massey, "restitution," *Holman Illustrated Bible Dictionary*, ed. by Trent C. Butler (Nashville: Holman Bible Publishers, 2003), 1379–80.

2. Guttmacher Institute, "Facts on Induced Abortion in the United States," In Brief: Fact Sheet, August 2011, www.guttmacher.org/pubs/fb_induced_abortion.html.

3. Rachel Jones, Rebecca Wind, and Heather Boonstra, "Most Important Reasons Given for Terminating an Unwanted Pregnancy," slide 12 of *An Overview of Abortion in the United States*, Guttmacher Institute, August 2011, accessed March 2, 2012, www.guttmacher.org/presentations.

4. John Ensor, author of *Answering the Call: Saving Innocent Lives One Woman at a Time* (Hendrickson Publishers, 2012), in an interview by Kim Jeffries (Ketola), "Along the Way," Faith Radio Network, St. Paul, MN, 2006.

5. Ibid.

KIM KETOLA, a writer and broadcaster with more than thirty years of radio and television experience in both the general market and for Christian audiences, is dedicated to helping others connect in faith to God, especially after abortion. She's most well known by her broadcast name of Kim Jeffries at CBS' WCCO Radio and Television, KTIS and Faith Radio Network, KS95, and *Life Redeemed*™, the radio and online outreach she hosted and produced to feature first-person stories of healing after abortion with expert commentary from leading Christian voices.

She's created, organized, and presented professionally-accredited conferences for healing after abortion (approved by the State of Minnesota for Licensed Psychologists, Social Workers, and Marriage and Family Therapists); she's traveled internationally, presenting postabortion workshops with Ruth Graham and Friends since 2007. For the annual national conferences of Heartbeat International and Lutherans for Life, she's served as faculty, and is a frequent keynote speaker, at churches and community events.

Kim studied communications at Northwestern University, and earned her Bachelor's degree in ministry from Northwestern College, where she also taught media ministry as adjunct faculty. Her commentaries have appeared in several publications, and she is a frequent media guest addressing pro-life issues on Salem, Moody, Sirius, and other network outlets.

Tim Pawlenty appointed Kim as chairperson of the Minnesota Governor's Council on Faith and Community Service Initiatives (2006–2008), and she has served many organizations reaching the homeless, the addict, and those in prison with a message about the love of Jesus Christ. She and her husband, Bruce, make their home in suburban Atlanta, where they welcome visits from their four young adult children.

Visit www.kimketola.com or www.cradlemyheart.org, where you will find more resources, including healing material specifically for men dealing with abortion.